BIG CATS OF THE WORLD

THE WORLD OF NATURE

BIG CATS OF THE WORLD

From the text of
GUIDO BADINO

With a foreword by
DR DESMOND MORRIS

BOUNTY BOOKS
A Division of Crown Publishers, Inc.,
NEW YORK

Title page: Allan Rose
Endpapers: Alan Weaving/Ardea Photographics

Copyright © 1975 by Istituto Geografico de Agostini, Novara
English edition © 1975 by Orbis Publishing Limited, London
Library of Congress Catalog card number: 74-78687
All rights reserved
This edition is published by Bounty Books
a division of Crown Publishers Inc.
by arrangement with Orbis Publishing Limited
a b c d e f g h
Printed in Italy by IGDA, Novara
Originally published in Italian as *I Felini*
Translated by Lt-Col James Heaton, FIL, TG

Foreword

Man has always been fascinated by the big cats, and it is a fascination born of a mixture of fear and admiration. If we concentrate our imagination on a giant feline form, hurtling towards us through the air, its flick-knife claws spread naked from its padded feet, its limb-muscles tense for a stunning blow, its crunching jaws impatient to plunge home its dagger teeth, we can be excused if, even in the warm security of our beds, we feel a wave of primeval panic pass through our bodies. If, instead, we picture the lazy, handsome, soft-bodied giant, yawning sleepily, sprawled half on its back, benignly tolerant of clumsy cubs pouncing on its tail, we feel not fear, but a warm glow of friendly respect.

It is these two conflicting feelings that have kept man's interest in the cat family so strongly alive for so many hundreds of years. The contradiction can even be found amongst children who have, as yet, only the slightest acquaintance with the family Felidae. When, during a television competition, young viewers were asked to name their top-ten animal likes and their top-ten animal dislikes, from all the wild creatures in the world, it was a member of the cat family that was the only animal to gain a place in both these top-ten lists. That animal was the lion – the eighth most liked and the third most disliked animal in the minds of these British children. Only a big cat could produce such a conflicting, double reaction.

Amongst fashionable women conflict looms again. There are those who love to wear the pelts of giant cats as glamour coats, and those who castigate them for doing so. The furriers' rich clients are behaving as though they are performing the last act in a grim ritual of primitive triumph, in which remnants of the vanquished are displayed as adornments on the bodies of tribal victors. To wear a leopard-skin coat is to claim a personal superiority over the departed cat. The opponents of these sophisticated savages point out that man's global superiority over all animal species is already so well established, that to continue to flay big cats merely for social display, when adequate substitutes are available, is a cowardly case of kicking a fauna when it is down.

To a zoologist like myself the situation is clear enough. Our ancient primate ancestors may often have fallen at a feline kill, but that was long ago. We must put aside our ancient antagonisms and fears of the giant killer-cats and adopt a more objective attitude. The time has come, not to exploit the surviving wild cat populations, but to help them—to offer aid before our erstwhile competitors are driven out of business by the spreading tide of 'Coca-Colonization', and become totally, genetically bankrupt. Surely, no one who has met a wild species of cat face-to-face can wish to see it and its relatives disappear completely from the crowded lands of this planet—even if its survival means handing over large virgin spaces that might otherwise be overrun by human occupation. There are so many millions of human beings on earth, and increasingly few wild felines. How far do we want to push our advantage? Do we really want to become a one-species planet? Unless we do something to correct the balance soon, it may, before very long, be too late.

Any book, like this one, that makes us think again about the splendour of that supreme peak of mammalian evolution we call the cat family, is a valuable book to publish and to own. It is worth possessing for the illustrations alone, but now that an English adaptation has been made from the original text, we can enjoy the words as well as the music—the magical visual music of tails and talons, eyes and fur, spots and stripes that we find when we enter the domain of those magnificent creatures—the wild cats of the world.

Desmond Morris

Contents

Index of cats

The cat family

Among the most familiar and best-loved of all animals are domestic cats. Partly for this reason, even those who take little interest in animals in general are easily able to recognize other members of the cat family when they see them. When visiting a zoo, looking at pictures, watching television, or—for the lucky few—when glimpsing wild cats in their natural surroundings, there is no difficulty in identifying any of them, be it a lion or a European wild cat, as a kind of cat. In so many ways cats of all kinds are alike.

That this should be so is not surprising, for all cats, whether wild or tame, are related to each other. In the distant past they shared common ancestors. They are distantly related and related animals, of course, tend to resemble each other.

To the zoologist the cats make up a single family, scientifically known as the family Felidae. In classifying animals the word 'family' is not used indiscriminately for any related group, as we tend to use it in ordinary conversation, when, for example, it may refer to just the parents and their young, while at other times, such as weddings and at Christmas, it may also include uncles, aunts, and second cousins. In zoological classification a family contains only animals which are, in the

Right: Serval (Felis serval). *Because the cats have fewer teeth than other carnivores, their jaws are shorter. This gives great power in biting. The carved, fang-like canine teeth are at the front of the mouth*

Jacana

Bruce Coleman/D. C. Houston

Marka

long perspective of evolutionary time, reasonably closely related. All members of the same family must be descended from the same ancestors who lived only a few millions, or at the most, tens of millions of years earlier. Animals even more closely related than this make up a smaller group within the family, scientifically known as a genus, which in turn contains even more closely-knit groups, the species.

Comparable to the cat family are the dog family and the bear family, which, together with other families, make up an even larger group of more distantly related animals, the order Carnivora. The zoologist defines the members of this order in terms of their evolutionary relationship, which is apparent because all members of the order tend to have a broad inherited resemblance to each other. As their name implies, the members of the order Carnivora are in the main meat-eaters. In its turn the order is grouped with others to make up a larger group, the class Mammalia, all the members of which, including man, share such features as the possession of hair, and are fed on milk when they are young.

Among the living members of Carnivora the cats are in many respects the most efficient and deadly of hunters. All the cat species are superbly adapted to hunting and killing their prey. They have keen senses, active bodies capable of both stealthy movement and powerful springing, and their teeth are deadly weapons. It is their deadly efficiency which makes the cats such fascinating animals to the human observer, as long as he or she does not become too closely involved!

The evolution and specialization of the larger carnivores has run parallel to the development of two other large groups of mammals—collectively known as the ungulates. These are herbivorous and include the most modern and successful of large herbivores, the ruminants. This parallel development is by no means a coincidence; there has always been a close interdependence between the two groups, and necessarily so, since the very survival of the large carnivores is dependent on the various species of ungulates which form their natural prey. Ecologists consider that the population of one group directly regulates that of the other. If the prey species becomes rare, then some of the predators will starve. If the prey species becomes numerous, then the abundant food will allow the predators to increase in numbers. The two populations must always be in a dynamic balance with each other. This enables the two groups to develop harmoniously, preventing over-population and keeping competition for food and living space within reasonable limits.

Above left: A cheetah cub (Acinonyx jubatus) *showing the characteristic rounded head*

Above: Leopard (Panthera pardus). *This species is very well adapted for a predatory life in forests and bush country*

Special adaptations

Within the Fissipedia the cats can in many respects be considered as the predators *par excellence*, and one demonstration of this can be found in their extremely specialized dentition, which is ideal for carnivorous use.

This specialization is evident from the shape of the teeth, some of which are ideally adapted for tearing their prey, while others are adapted for reducing it into smaller pieces. Cats have fewer teeth than any other members of the Carnivora, and because of this they have shorter jaws and can therefore bite harder in proportion to their size.

We can compare, for instance, the dentition of a lion (one of the cats) with that of a wolf (a member of the dog family) which is also a member of the Fissipedia, by first examining the respective dental formulae and then the detail of each set of teeth.

The dental formula for the lion is:

$I\frac{3}{3}$, $C\frac{1}{1}$, $P\frac{3}{2}$, $M\frac{1}{1}$.

For the wolf it is:

$I\frac{3}{3}$, $C\frac{1}{1}$, $P\frac{4}{4}$, $M\frac{2}{3}$.

In these formulae I refers to the incisors, C to the canines, P to the premolars and M to the molars. The top figures refer to the upper jaw and the bottom figures to the lower jaw. The numbers of teeth given are for one side of the jaws only.

It is evident from the formulae that the lion

A lioness. The digitigrade paws enable the big cats to move silently and with an extremely light tread. They are always on 'tip-toe'

Marka

3

has fewer premolars and molars, the teeth used for the crushing and shearing of food, than has the wolf. This marked decrease in molars necessarily leads to a shortening of the jaw and a less protruberant muzzle, which results in the head taking on a more rounded appearance, accentuated even further by the presence of highly developed jaw muscles on either side. An additional point of interest is that the joint between the lower jaw and skull is sufficiently large to allow the cat to open its mouth as wide as is necessary in order to kill its prey.

The canines, which are sharp in all the carnivores, are tusk-like in the lion and all the cat family, pointed but still relatively powerful. The hindmost of the three premolars in the upper jaw and the first molar in the lower jaw, which meet when the mouth is closed, are highly developed in all living members of the Fissipedia and are known as carnassial teeth. They are the largest and the most important of the chewing teeth.

In the cat these carnassial or flesh-tearing teeth are specially developed and have three tough, triangular cusps. The solitary upper molar, on the other hand, is extremely rudimentary.

These large tearing teeth clearly illustrate the perfect adaptation of the cat family to strictly carnivorous feeding habits. Their carnassial teeth

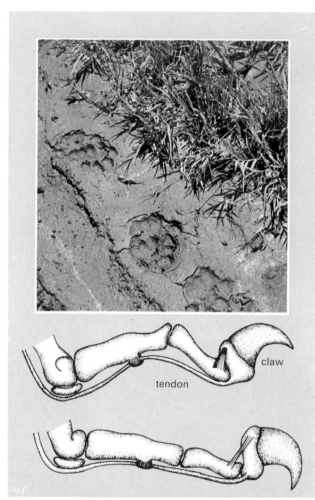

Above left: The track of a lion

Left: This sketch illustrates the retractile mechanism of a cat's claw

Left: A lion cub. The thick horny covering on the pads of the feet is clearly visible

strongly contrast with those found among the bears, which are related to the cats, and, like them, are members of the Fissipedia. Bears have omnivorous feeding habits, and their carnassial teeth have lost their importance as flesh cutters. They have low, bumpy cusps not dissimilar to those of other omnivorous mammals such as man.

Although most cats can run swiftly, they do not normally run over very great distances but lie in ambush to catch their prey. The musculature and skeletal structure of the limbs have become specialized for this purpose. The overall shape of the limbs enables the cat to creep up very close to its unsuspecting prey before finally lunging swiftly forward and taking the unwitting victim by surprise.

In the cat family, paws are completely digitigrade, which means that the cats walk on tip-toe. This effectively makes the legs longer and permits rapid movement. There are five toes on the forefeet, although the first one (which corresponds to the human thumb) is set higher than the rest and does not reach the ground, and four toes on the hind feet, the first toe (corresponding to the human big toe) being absent. The digitigrade arrangement can certainly be accepted as one of the most efficient evolutionary mechanisms for light, springy and therefore swift movement. This

A leopard (right), a cheetah (below), and a lioness (below right). In each case the full crowns of their flesh-shearing teeth can be clearly seen

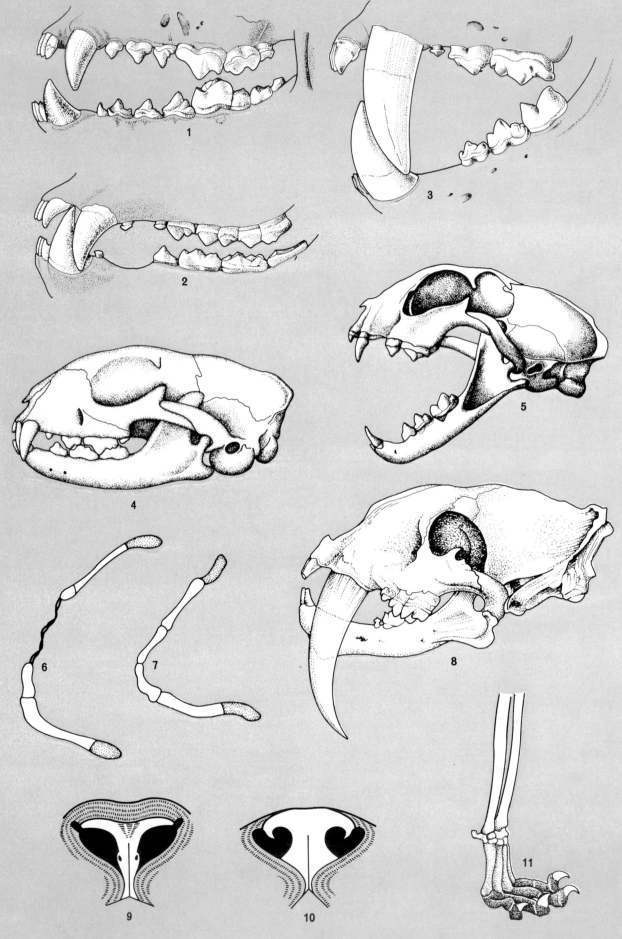

can be illustrated by the observation that, although humans walk on flat feet, we rise on to our toes when we run or jump.

The reduction in the number of digits and the posterior deplacement of two of them (the second and fourth in the hind feet) has the advantage of decreasing the bearing surface of the paw, thus enabling the animal to move over the ground with reduced abrasion.

This adaptation of the paws for rapid movement has been further accentuated by the curved claws which are normally retracted into protective sheaths at the ends of the digits. This action is facilitated by a somewhat complex system of small tendons, pliable ligaments and muscles, which control the reciprocal movements of each separate bone in the digit. Because they are retracted the claws are not worn and blunted during ordinary movement as are those of other animals, such as dogs. Finally, on the under-surface of the foot there is one pad at the base of each digit, and one larger pad in the middle. These soft pads enable the cat to move silently.

The cheetah (*Acinonyx jubatus*) is the only large cat which will often capture its prey after pursuing it for some hundreds of yards. It is found in Africa, Asia Minor and India. From an anatomical viewpoint, its slender graceful body enables the maximum amount of power to be translated into movement, and its non-retractile claws maximize its speed. For the cheetah, speed in pursuit is more important than stealth, and its claws grip the ground, functioning in the same way as the spiked running shoes of an athlete. Because of its speed it was tamed in India and used for antelope hunting, though, of course, more in the past than nowadays.

Cats often hunt at night as in the dark they possess a great advantage over some other animals. This is due to their acute eyesight, very delicate sense of hearing and good sense of smell.

It is not true that cats can see in the dark, but they can certainly see in very dim light. Who has not seen the glint of a cat's eye in the night? This is due to the special characteristics of the choroid, the vascular coat lining the eyeball, which in many of the other vertebrates is heavily pigmented. The choroid of the cat, however, has an exceptional capacity for reflection. It works like a mirror, since the cellular layer nearest the retina (the sensitive nerve layer of the eye) is composed of fibrous elements which reflect light. The weak, night light impinging on the retina is reflected from the choroid, enabling the cells of the retina to catch stronger visual images. Because it is reflected, each ray of light has two chances to stimulate the eye. Within the cellular structure of

the retina, the light-sensitive rods predominate—these cells occurring in great numbers in all the vertebrates whose activity is mainly nocturnal. Animals which are more active in daylight, on the other hand, have a large proportion of cone-shaped cells which function only in bright light but which are capable of producing a sharper, more detailed image.

The tactile vibrissae, commonly known as whiskers, are situated on the front of the muzzle, mainly near the nose. They are specially developed hairs, with a specific sensory function, although they are not true sense organs. Nevertheless, they do give the animal a good tactile perception of near objects. The numerous cutaneous nerve endings situated at the base of the whiskers transmit every mechanical stimulation picked up by the vibrissae themselves.

While the cat's sense of smell is not the predominant sense, it is a strong one. The special structure of the nose itself and the highly developed olfactory centre in the brain enable the animal to receive and elaborate even a very faint odour.

Below: In the smaller members of the cat family, the pupils contract in strong light and become narrow vertical slits

ZEFA

Cats in danger of extinction

Below: The cheetah (Acinonyx jubatus) has now completely disappeared from India. It is rare in other former Asian strongholds, and is declining in numbers in Africa. It will probably become completely extinct unless very strong measures are taken to ensure its survival

Because of the perfected anatomical, nutritional and behavioural aspects that have developed during the course of evolution, one might imagine that the big cats would be more widely distributed than they in fact are, and that their relative numbers would rapidly increase.

Although widely distributed (except in Australia and Madagascar), it is sad but undeniably true that almost all of the carnivores, and certainly all cats living in the wild, are decreasing in numbers, and some species are desperately close to extinction. Most people know of the Spanish lynx which has now practically disappeared. Unfortunately the same situation is occurring with the cheetah, and this animal is now in grave danger in both Africa and India. This depletion can be almost entirely attributed to the destructive actions of man. Man is blinded, either by superstition or by a preconceived notion that predatory animals are dangerous. He can sometimes be spurred to destroy by a desire for the gain from the sale of some coveted multi-coloured coat or, worse still, be drawn on by the need to assuage some innate predatory urge of his own. This

Ardea Photographics / R. Waller

destructive action on the part of man has, in a relatively short space of time, in some respects wiped out the slow but effective work which natural selection has been doing for millions of years in favour of the cat family.

Ill-considered hunting is a dangerous intrusion into the delicate equilibrium which regulates the relationship between animals. All big cats in India, Africa or the Americas represent an invaluable element in the maintenance of this equilibrium.

What are the consequences of these disturbances created by man? Already we have seen that their effects reinforce our worst fears and stress the need for active protection of the so-called 'dangerous' animals. Dorst has illustrated this point in his reference to the destruction of the puma and the lynx in the western United States, because of the damage they caused to flocks and herds. The decrease in the number of pumas and lynxes very quickly resulted in a massive proliferation of the rodents normally hunted by these cats. The farmers then turned their attention to this new menace, while the pumas and lynxes were afforded a respite. The latter returned, but no longer finding their natural prey, which had been decimated by man, once more attacked the domestic cattle, this time producing far more damage than in their earlier depredations which had sparked off the whole train of events.

The leopard, too, is fast disappearing from vast areas of both Africa and Asia. Although there has been considerable legislation to protect the leopard, it is often ineffective and the animal is being hunted, often indiscriminately, in order to supply the international market with highly priced furs. The destruction of the leopard has obviously resulted in an overwhelming increase in their

Below: At least six of the eight subspecies of the tiger (Panthera tigris) *are in grave danger of extinction*

natural prey, such as warthogs and baboons, which now invade cultivated areas and cause enormous damage. It seems obvious, then, that more positive efforts to protect the leopard need to be made. There must be more effective control over the hunting of this animal and perhaps greater encouragement should be given to safaris with cameras, instead of those with guns.

The Indian lion (*Panthera leo persica*) has also been decimated by man, in efforts to protect his cattle, and today less than 280 of these animals remain, confined to the Forest of Gir in India. They are now so few in number that they cannot fulfil their ecological role of maintaining a natural equilibrium in the population of wild herbivores, such as deer, which in any event have been replaced by man's goats and cattle. As a result of human greed the goats have increased at an alarming rate, devouring the tender saplings and so preventing normal forest regrowth. The whole delicately balanced ecology of the area is threatened.

These examples clearly indicate that the reduction in numbers of any one member of the community is liable to have an incalculable result on the environment as a whole.

Though it seems paradoxical, we can agree with Ziswiler that the presence of a sufficient number of predators is actually an indispensable factor for the survival of their natural prey. In support of this view we may cite as evidence an event which occurred recently in a hunting reserve in Arizona. Here, in attempting to ensure the survival of the deer, the authorities decided to get rid of all the predators they could find, especially the puma. Without natural enemies the deer reproduced and multiplied to a disastrous extent and, with the increased pressure on food,

Below: The Asiatic lion (Panthera leo persica) *is the only representative of the species now surviving outside the African continent. Not many more than a hundred animals survive, and these are actively protected in the Forest of Gir National Park, in India*

11

much of the vegetation in the reserve was destroyed. This meant that the deer's particular fodder became pitifully short, serious pestilence broke out and the herd was finally reduced to only a few animals.

We know that predators usually attack the oldest or youngest, and weak or sick animals, which move more slowly and naturally offer less resistance. It follows that the predators tend to eliminate the less healthy animals from a herd, and thus help maintain a vigorous population. Here, again, we see natural selection working harmoniously, and we can see how easily it can be upset.

Protective Measures

To combat the present difficulties we have discussed, there are many organizations actively concerned with wildlife protection, and cam-

paigns are now being conducted to save those species which are at present in any danger of extinction.

Awareness of the ecological situation is now becoming more and more acute, and the number of game parks and nature reserves is on the increase—especially in Africa. The interested African countries are introducing specific measures to protect the big cats, as are governments all over the world. The United States, for example, has recently given a pledge not to import the skins of those big cats which are in danger of extinction. These include the Asian cheetah, all the subspecies of the tiger and leopard, the snow leopard, the clouded leopard, the jaguar and the ocelot. Great Britain has also banned the import of skins of tigers, the snow leopard and the clouded leopard, and has imposed controls on leopard and cheetah skins. This decision is of

Above left: A clouded leopard cub (Panthera nebulosa), *a few months old. This animal, which in appearance is one of the most attractive of all the cats, is now in danger of extinction*

Above: Indian tiger. This animal is now considered to be off the 'danger list' due to its protection in numerous national parks and integrated nature reserves

particular importance as England is one of the most important centres for the fur trade in the world.

Over the entrances to the reserves of the Wildfowl Trust at Slimbridge and Peakirk in Great Britain is written: 'No entry to those wearing genuine fur of spotted cats or tigers. This policy has been adopted by the Wildfowl Trust in support of the campaign of the World Wildlife Fund to prevent the extinction of these animals.'

The W.W.F. (World Wildlife Fund), an international society for the protection of the environment, and the International Federation for Trade in Furs (I.F.T.F.), completed an agreement on 10 September 1971 prohibiting commerce in tiger, snow leopard and clouded leopard skins.

Perhaps an even greater reason for man's decimation of the cat population, however, is the pressure of civilized agriculture on land use. In

historical times man has been responsible in this way for the extinction of at least four varieties of big cats. These are: the European lion, which disappeared from Greece in the first or second century AD; the eastern race of the puma, which has become extinct during this century in the eastern United States; the Cape lion, the last specimen of which was killed in South Africa in 1865, and the Barbary lion, which disappeared from North Africa in 1922.

It may be useful at this point to give a complete list of all the varieties of big cats now facing the possibility of extinction: Indian cheetah, African cheetah, Javanese tiger, Balinese tiger, Caspian tiger (Northern Iran and Turkestan), Lop Nor tiger (Chinese Turkestan), Siberian tiger (Siberian region of Amur and Ussuri), Indian lion (Forest of Gir), North African caracal, and the Spanish lynx (Sierra Morena, southern Spain).

Man and the cat family

It is undeniable that man himself is the greatest enemy of the wild cats. It may be suggested that the indiscriminate destruction of these animals is a justifiable reaction by man against the danger these beasts present. Are the tales that we hear of 'man-eating tigers', or of wild animals attacking man, really true, or are they simply legends? There still remain many preconceptions on this subject which need to be discredited.

All wild animals, including cats, are, in general, afraid of man and the local population is usually aware of this fact. Animals normally flee man's presence, unless it is physically impossible for them to do so.

The relationship between animal and trainer in the circus is basic proof of this fear. Only the impossibility of escaping from a desperate situation, coupled with the strong instinct for survival, will drive a big cat to overcome this basic fear.

It does happen—for example when their natural prey is less easy to find—that older wild cats will sometimes attack domesticated herds or flocks of animals and so become a real menace to isolated herdsmen. It must be stressed, however, that the wild animals which roam round villages and, when hungry, attack men, are 'desperate' animals. They have been forced to leave the security of their homes in the wild because they are old and no longer capable of competing with younger animals in the hunt for their natural prey. But often, even before reaching a village, these older animals themselves fall victims to their own natural enemies. The hyaena, for example, will attack an old lion, or any other species of the cat family living in the same regions. It is by no means rare for an elderly male lion to wander away from the pride, followed by hyaenas, and, when finally exhausted, to surrender to their attacks.

An event which occurred in the spring of 1962 on the high crater of Ngorongoro, in Tanzania, is of much interest as an illustration of how, in really exceptional circumstances, cats are motivated to penetrate some villages. In that year particularly humid conditions led to a surprising increase in the numbers of bloodsucking flies (*Stomoxys calcitrans*). The lions were tormented beyond endurance and blindly attempted to escape in every way possible. Driven from their normal hunting grounds, they turned on the Masai villages and attacked the domestic cattle.

Another question is repeatedly asked: if the wild beasts are afraid of man, why does he have to hunt them when the need to use them for food does not arise? There are two straightforward answers. One is that they may attack his herds, the second is that they compete with man in the hunt for wild game. However, there may be less tangible reasons. It might well be that from time immemorial man has seen the beast as a symbol of aggression and of the mysterious power of

Right: Cheetah (Acinonyx jubatus). Below: A melanistic leopard or black panther (Panthera pardus). Despite their forbidding appearance, the big cats rarely attack man, and then only in conditions of extreme necessity

Animals-Animals/Z. Lesz

14

Bruce Coleman/Sher Jang Singh

Left: Tiger in the jungle undergrowth. Although there are many legends of 'man-eating' tigers, cats of this species will not normally attack man

natural forces and, in the final analysis, the killer of the wild beast becomes himself the possessor of what this symbol represents. This recalls the pictures of native medicine men disguised in leopard skins and other trophies of the hunt, and it certainly seems to have been the force behind the cult of the jaguar in Ancient Mexico. This transposition confers a kind of magical potency, which undoubtedly arises from the belief of having acquired, in some manner, the spirit of the 'beast' which has been slaughtered.

As we have noticed, however, it is not only medicine men who find the coats attractive, and, since the coat is an important factor in the relationship between man and the cat family, it is perhaps worth examining in greater detail here.

In every case the design, or simply the colour alone, of the cat's coat possesses, in common with its other bodily characteristics, an adaptive

Bruce Coleman/Sher Jang Singh

Left: White tigers occur only very occasionally in nature. In captivity, they have been bred from the descendants of a white tiger captured in the principality of Rewa, in India. Some fine examples of white tigers can be seen in Bristol Zoo, England

E. Hosking

Above: The lion (Panthera leo) becomes irritable and intractable during the mating period, and may then present a danger to man

significance. In relation to its environment it has a unique protective function as camouflage, enabling the cat to carry out surprise attacks on its prey.

The species with spotted coats are usually found in forest regions, and we can quote a few examples. The leopard (*Panthera pardus*) usually has dark rosettes on a brown background and lives in the deep tropical forests and bush country of Africa and Asia. It does sometimes move into more open, but still wooded, areas. The fishing cat (*Felis viverrina*) with its tawny coat covered with large darker-coloured spots, lives in the marshy Asian forests. The clouded leopard (*Panthera nebulosa*) has a yellowish coat with large, dark, ring-like grey spots, enabling it to blend with the shadows of the trees of the South-East Asian forests. Finally, as an example of a tropical American species, the ocelot (*Felis pardalis*), with its spotted fur, lives in the wooded zones of Central and South America.

The coat of the tiger (*Panthera tigris*) reveals protective colouring *par excellence*, being tawny with large black stripes. The beast's silhouette perfectly harmonizes with the interplay of light and shade which dominates the jungle twilight, so that the tiger can silently creep forward to within 10 m (30 feet) of his unsuspecting prey

before finally attacking in a great leap. It blends equally well with the shadows of Asia's more open, grassy jungles. On the other hand, in a featureless, dry, brown environment like the savanna—the habitat of the lion (*Panthera leo*) the animal's coat is a predominantly tawny colour. Even here the harmony between the dominant shades of colour of the environment (the yellowish-brown sunburnt vegetation), and the colour of the cat inhabiting it, is without doubt quite perfect. This uniformity of colour also occurs in the puma (*Felis concolor*), which inhabits, among other places, the North American prairies.

Melanism is a frequent occurrence in some species of wild cats. Melanistic individuals have almost uniformly dark fur, as happens in the case of the so-called black panther, which is really nothing more than a melanistic leopard. Cases of erythrism (or a tendency towards reddish fur) also occur, and we have a good example near us in the case of the common domestic cat with red fur. We sometimes even find animals with albinism—where the melanin pigment is completely absent, or is only sparse. These phenomena can all occur in the tiger (*Panthera tigris*). 'White' tigers have almost white fur, with brown stripes, and have blue eyes.

17

Reproduction

In the domestic cat we have a rich and convenient source for a study of the physiology and behaviour patterns of the cats in reproduction. The female normally has more than one period of oestrus or 'heat' during the course of the year, and is usually ready for mating in both spring and autumn. In this respect tame cats differ from such species as the European wild cat, where the females experience oestrus in the spring only.

During the oestrus period, one or more of the ovarian follicles mature, and the female is ready for fertilization. The small endocrine gland known as the pituitary body, situated at the base of the brain, triggers the whole range of phenomena characteristic of the oestrus period, producing specific hormones and secreting substances into the blood stream which stimulate the ovaries. In species which have a definite breeding season this process is governed by specific environmental conditions such as light and temperature.

In the cat family, with few exceptions, male and female stay apart for most of the year and only come together during the courtship period.

Below: A pair of Siberian tigers (Panthera tigris altaica). During the courtship rituals, tenderness and violent quarrels alternate. These are usually provoked by the female

Jacana/W. Schraml

To let the males know that they are ready for mating, the females indicate their condition by leaving their urine in various parts of the territory (that area individuals or groups normally defend against other members of the species). During the 'heat' period in fact, the odorous perineal glands begin to function, and these impart a special smell to the urine, clearly apparent to the male. The female, for her part, becomes acutely aware of the male's presence. A system of social communication comes into play which can be considered to be 'chemical' in so far as it consists of specific, volatile, and odorous male secretions known to the zoologist as 'phermones'. These act as a stimulus to the female. Simultaneous stimulation in both sexes is the essential prelude to the ritual courtship.

This particular stimulatory mechanism has been reproduced in the laboratory by acting on the nerve centres of the olfactory system (the olfactory lobe in the brain). This results in the production of abundant vaginal secretions, similar to those which would occur in natural conditions during the courtship ritual.

Following a more or less complex courtship, which may vary considerably in its duration and which to the human observer often looks extremely ferocious, a brief coupling occurs, which is almost always repeated several times.

In the cats which make up the genus *Panthera*, which comprises all the really big cats, the female squats docilely, often making deep, low-pitched yowling noises, and the male mounts on her back gripping her by the scruff of the neck with his teeth. Desmond Morris considers that although the bite appears to indicate violence on the part of the male, it is really the equivalent of our maternal embrace. He points out that the bite is controlled so that the teeth do not actually harm the female, and that this is the method by which the adult carnivores carry their young from one place to another. Thus the male is really treating the female like a cub. If she is sexually responsive to his approach, Morris maintains, this is exactly how she does act, offering her neck to her partner's jaws as she formerly offered it to her mother.

Ovulation usually follows mating and is

Below: Although lion cubs are usually weaned by the time they are eight or nine months old, they only start to become independent of the mother when they are a year old and the permanent teeth have appeared

E. Hosking

Bruce Coleman/M. Quraishy

Ardea Photographics/C. Weaver

actually induced by it; in the domestic cat it occurs in 26 hours and the fertilized eggs in the oviduct move slowly down towards the uterus, which they reach on the sixth day. For a week they remain free in the uterus, and implantation in the uterine mucosa takes place only 13 days after mating. The phenomenon of ovulation immediately following the coupling of the animals is considered to be an important adaptive mechanism ensuring that the reproductive processes function in the most efficient manner possible. It is by no means exclusive to the Felidae, and has been verified in other mammals such as the rabbit and ferret.

The impulse to the ovary for the follicle to rupture and release the ovum is controlled by hormones; again this is a pituitary action, mediated by the hypothalamus. When males are absent, the follicles in the female cat decrease in

Above: When about six weeks old the young cheetahs leave the lair to follow their mother and begin the long apprenticeship which enables them to become skilled hunters

Above right: A pair of cheetahs exchanging affectionate nuzzles in the vast, unchanging stretches of the savanna

20

volume and degenerate. Following experimental removal of the pituitary body the female no longer ovulates, even when she is being mated regularly.

The period of gestation varies according to species: two months for the smaller cats of the genus *Felis*, three months for the puma (*Felis concolor*), 93–110 days for the jaguar (*Panthera onca*), 105–110 days for the tiger (*Panthera tigris*), 105–113 for the lion (*Panthera leo*), and around 95 days for the cheetah (*Acinonyx jubatus*). The size of litter also varies. The lioness has between one and six cubs, usually three or four at each birth, and all the big cats of the genus *Panthera* follow this pattern. The female cheetah has two to four, and the females of the genus *Felis* usually have from one to six kittens.

The young are almost always born blind and are at first unable to walk, but they are already well covered with fur. Their coats may be significantly different in colour from those of their parents. This happens not only with the puma and lion, but also with the cheetah whose young have thick manes, extending from the head down the whole length of the back to the tail, leaving only the flanks and paws which already show the typical spotted pattern of the adult. Minor differences appear in the leopard cubs, which have a greyish coat, already completely spotted in black.

In zoos it is sometimes possible to overcome those barriers of incompatibility inherent in the species and interbreed animals of different species, obtaining hybrids with intermediate characteristics—although it seems that they are always sterile. Some examples of these are the results obtained when lions are crossed with tigers. If the father is a lion, the offspring is known as a liger, and if the father is a tiger then it is called a tigon.

Origins and classification

By examining the evidence of fossil remains, it is possible to reconstruct the evolutionary development of the cat family. It is quite clear that the present cat family constitutes an extremely homogeneous group, both from an anatomical viewpoint and in other ways. For example, all living cats have very similar chromosomes, the microscopic thread-like structures which make up the nucleus of each cell. With the exception of two species, all the cats studied have 38 chromosomes present, while the two exceptions, the ocelot (*Felis pardalis*), and the margay (*F. wiedi*)

differ only slightly, having just 36 chromosomes.

As with all the carnivores, the origin of the cats goes back to the family Miacidae, which populated North America in the first Eocene epoch (about 65 million years ago) and later passed over what used to be the Bering Isthmus into Eurasia. These animals were small carnivores and less specialized than modern cats. In strata of the Oligocene epoch (about 40 million years ago), fossilized remains of the true cats, originating from the Eocene stock common to all the carnivores, have been found. They were predators

Below: In the wild, the ranges of tigers and lions do not overlap, but in captivity they have been interbred. Like mules, however, both the liger and the tigon are sterile

Jacana/Frédrick

Right: Female leopard with her young. A devoted mother, the female leopard defends her cubs even in situations where females of other species might be induced to abandon their young

with a highly specialized dentition and they fall into two groups. Firstly the family Machairo-dontinae, which had developed long, sabre-like upper canines, while their lower canines had disappeared. Secondly, the cats, in the strict sense of the word, who already closely resembled, in other ways besides dentition, the present-day cats. During the Pleistocene era (about two million years ago), the Machairodontinae became extinct simultaneously in Europe, Asia and America—the reason why is still not known—leaving the family of cats which we now know.

For the subdivision of the cat family into genera and species, reference has been made to the classic 'Traité de Zoologie', edited by P. Grassé. In the chapter devoted to cats, the author divides them into only the three genera *Felis, Panthera*, and *Acinonyx*.

This view has the merit of simplicity, but it is not accepted by all experts. Like most other living things, the cats were first classified by Linnaeus, who placed all of them into the single genus *Felis*. In the years that followed zoologists split this group into smaller ones, until by about 50 years ago over 20 genera of cats had been named. A reaction against such extreme splitting then occurred, and the majority of zoologists lumped the genera together again, using the classification adopted by Grassé. However, there is now a tendency to use rather more genera. For example, the clouded leopard is not felt to fit neatly into either the genus *Panthera* or the genus *Felis*, and some zoologists have therefore resurrected the genus *Neofelis* for it. The lynxes are often now placed in their own separate genus (*Lynx*). Since the name of the genus forms the first part of the scientific name of the species, it is often useful to know the alternative generic names that may be encountered. For this reason the various generic names of cats used by those inclined to split them into smaller genera are given in the table on page 25.

In the classification used in this book, the genus *Felis* contains the greatest number of species, while the genus *Panthera* includes all the big cats except the one species of the third genus *Acinonyx*, which is the cheetah (*A. jubatus*).

The genus *Felis* includes small and medium sized cats with one particular feature in common, namely the complete ossification of the suspensory apparatus of the hyoid bone (the bone which supports the tongue), with the larynx restricted in movement in relation to the skull. All the species of this genus have retractile claws. There is no need to go into detail here, since the illustrations on page 6 provide the required information and it is sufficient to say that the domestic cat is included in this genus.

The genus *Panthera* comprises the bigger cats: the lion (*P. leo*), the tiger (*P. tigris*), the leopard (*P. pardus*), the snow leopard (*P. uncia*), the clouded leopard (*P. nebulosa*), and the jaguar (*P. onca*). As in the preceding genus, all these cats have retractile claws. The unique distinguishing characteristic is again the suspensory apparatus of the hyoid bone which, in the genus *Panthera*, is incompletely ossified, permitting greater movement of the larynx.

In the genus *Acinonyx* the characteristics of the hyoid apparatus are most like those of the genus *Felis*, but in *Acinonyx* the claws are not retractile in the adult, and this is why it must be considered as a separate genus.

The degree of mobility of the larynx, as already explained, is dependent on the level of ossification of the hyoid bone supporting the vocal apparatus, and this conditions the power of the voice in each species. The voice, therefore, is also a useful distinguishing characteristic.

All the species within the genus *Panthera*, such

Below: Continually alert to all around them, the cheetahs slake their thirst in one of the rare stretches of water in the savanna

as the lion and tiger, possess a powerful roar, all the more terrifying when the tremendous size of these big cats is considered. The lion's roar can be heard from a distance of 8 km (five miles).

The small cats of the genus *Felis*, however, have relatively weak voices, and these can range from a high-pitched yowl to a shrill or even pitiful 'miaow'.

Although it is not universally accepted, for the sake of completeness we include the following note on the more modern classification adopted by Grzimek (1972), in which the family Felidae is divided into two sub-families: the Nimravinae, now extinct, and the Felinae, which is further sub-divided into two tribes, one containing the genera *Felis* and *Panthera*, and the other the genus *Acinonyx*, to which the cheetah belongs. The first of these is further subdivided into a number of genera.

Right: Cheetah (Acinonyx jubatus). This species is adapted to life on the open plains, where it can make full use of its unique speed as a hunting technique. It has a slender body, long legs and small paws, with the non-retractile claws facilitating the animal's grip on the ground

Below right: One of the most beautiful cats in the African savanna, the serval (Felis serval)

Ardea Photographics / M. D. England

Bruce Coleman / N. Myers

Alternative generic names of cats used by some authorities			
English name	**Genus adopted in this book**	**Alternative generic name**	**Species**
Domestic cat	*Felis*	—	*catus*
European wild cat	*Felis*	—	*silvestris*
African wild cat	*Felis*	—	*libyca*
Sand cat	*Felis*	—	*margarita*
Black-footed cat	*Felis*	—	*nigripes*
Jungle cat	*Felis*	—	*chaus*
Pallas's cat	*Felis*	*Otocolobus*	*manul*
Serval	*Felis*	*Leptailurus*	*serval*
Lynx	*Felis*	*Lynx*	*lynx*
Canadian lynx	*Felis*	*Lynx*	*canadensis*
Bobcat	*Felis*	*Lynx*	*rufa*
Caracal lynx	*Felis*	*Lynx*	*caracal*
African golden cat	*Felis*	*Profelis*	*aurata*
Temminck's golden cat	*Felis*	*Profelis*	*temmincki*
Bay cat	*Felis*	*Profelis*	*badia*
Leopard cat	*Felis*	*Prionailurus*	*bengalensis*
Rusty-spotted cat	*Felis*	*Prionailurus*	*rubiginosa*
Fishing cat	*Felis*	*Prionailurus*	*viverrina*
Flat-headed cat	*Felis*	*Ictailurus*	*planiceps*
Marbled cat	*Felis*	*Pardofelis*	*marmorata*
Ocelot	*Felis*	*Leopardus*	*pardalis*
Margay	*Felis*	*Leopardus*	*wiedi*
Tiger cat	*Felis*	*Leopardus*	*tigrina*
Geoffroy's cat	*Felis*	*Leopardus*	*geoffroyi*
Kodkod	*Felis*	*Leopardus*	*guigna*
Pampas cat	*Felis*	*Lynchailurus*	*colocolo*
Mountain cat	*Felis*	*Oreailurus*	*jacobita*
Jaguarundi	*Felis*	*Herpailurus*	*yagouaroundi*
Puma	*Felis*	*Puma*	*concolor*
Clouded leopard	*Panthera*	*Neofelis*	*nebulosa*
Snow leopard or ounce	*Panthera*	*Uncia*	*uncia*
Leopard	*Panthera*	—	*pardus*
Jaguar	*Panthera*	—	*onca*
Tiger	*Panthera*	—	*tigris*
Lion	*Panthera*	—	*leo*
Cheetah	*Acinonyx*	—	*jubatus*

Aggression and predatory behaviour

Although to human eyes the wild cats appear to be exceptionally fierce, they are no more aggressive than any other animals. The tiger's attitude towards its prey is no more aggressive than that of a donkey towards a tasty thistle. It is true that cats hunt and kill other animals, but they do so only in order to obtain food. Their predatory behaviour is spurred by a feeling of hunger and reaches its climax when the prey, in mortal fear, takes to its heels and flees as fast as possible.

The attack unfolds in a sequence of movements which differs slightly from one species to another and is often also influenced by the behaviour of the prey. In any event, the hunting technique has been gradually refined during the evolution of

each species of cat, and it seems that, in their broad outlines, the techniques have become hereditary and are transmitted from generation to generation.

Nevertheless, it is still very important for each individual animal to learn all it can from its mother and from its own experience. For example, the young animal may have inherited from birth the tendency to notice and seize anything that moves, but it will still need parental guidance in order to perfect the best techniques for surprising its prey, seizing it, quickly immobilizing it and finally killing it.

The young animals stay with their parents for long periods, in some cases for more than a year.

Below: Like most of the big cats, the lion kills its prey by sinking its teeth into the neck of its victim and breaking the cervical vertebrae. In the picture immediately below one can see the head of the zebra, which seems to be still alive, but shortly afterwards (below right) the neck is broken and the head lolls on one side

Ardea Photographics / J. S. Wightman

This is not merely for protection in an environment where the struggle for survival is often dramatic, but also because of the great need to learn to hunt with cunning—a skill which has to be perfected by the young animal before it is able to fend for itself. It is also necessary, of course, in order to allow for maturation to take place, the animal having to attain a certain size and strength before it is able to kill its prey. Finally, this period provides the opportunity to play with the other young cubs within the family group, which is essential to the development of adult behaviour patterns.

In order to assess the relative importance of hereditary factors and acquired skills in the predatory behaviour of a cat, the young of wild animal species have been reared in experimental isolation, before any of them have had experience in catching live prey. Under these conditions, when brought face to face with, for example, a live rodent, the young at first show interest in the animal, though without actually attacking it so long as it does not attempt to escape. A moving object, on the other hand, provides the required stimulus and triggers instinctive behaviour for attack and seizure of the prey. But before the young animals learn to seize and kill their prey correctly, they go through a long period of trial and error, only gradually perfecting the necessary sequence of actions.

Learning would seem, therefore, to be an indispensable element in refining and correcting the cat's movements until a positive result is achieved. However, some workers in this field consider that there is a hereditary component which predisposes a species to learn the particular behavioural patterns and actions most suitable for eventually catching their prey. If this is true, then the process that has been observed is perhaps better regarded as one of maturation.

The most generalized form of hunting technique is the surprise attack where either the prey is ambushed, or the predator creeps up in a succession of stealthy approaches, getting nearer and nearer to the chosen victim before finally leaping onto it. Both big and small cats use these methods, as all are capable of great leaps forward, either from the ground or a tree branch, and of extremely rapid bursts of speed over short distances. However, none of the cats can sustain a lengthy chase, and even the cheetah, which often catches its prey in flight, does not normally keep up the chase for any distance greater than about 400 m ($\frac{1}{4}$ mile) at a time.

When lions come into conflict threatening postures and a formidable appearance are used as signals. These instinctive behaviour patterns are used in what is essentially a game of bluff. Usually, one of the contestants submits before serious damage is done

29

The prey is usually struck down and immobilized in one leap when, with the weight of their bodies and one blow of the forepaw, the big cats may actually stun the herbivores by breaking the neck, with consequent limb paralysis. In the final act of the killing technique, the big cats frequently seize their victims by the throat and, using their curved canine teeth, tear open the large blood vessels in the neck.

While aggression in the technical sense of the word plays no part in the predatory behaviour of the cats, it certainly plays an important role in the social relationships between animals of the same species. In particular, it regulates the attitudes and behaviour of each individual both within the confines of its own territory, and in relation to individuals or groups of its own species. It even plays some part in the courtship rituals which precede the act of mating.

In practice most wild cats exhibit territorial behaviour. This means that the area occupied by the population of a given species is divided into a number of territories depending on the number of individuals or groups of animals comprising the population. Within this territory the social unit hunts and reproduces.

This living space must be sufficiently large to provide adequate prey for the predators and their young, but may be further extended, depending on the degree of aggression shown by the animal or animals defending it, and the extent to which intruders are expelled. The territory can be defined as the area within which the impulse to attack other individuals of the same species, or in the case of social animals, members of rival groups of the same species, is stronger than the impulse to flee. The limits of the territory are often marked in some way, for example by

ZEFA

Left: Young cheetahs are born during the rainy season. They start to eat meat at the beginning of the dry season, when there are still plenty of young herbivores to afford an abundant supply of prey

Above: During mating, the lioness does not always look as if she welcomes the bite, albeit restrained, of the male

hold the ears close to the top of the head. This menacing posture, which in many instances is all that is necessary to avoid fighting, is an example of a most useful 'social signal', since it informs the intruder that it is encroaching on the defender's territory. The response can, and does, vary, depending on the intensity of the aggressive impulse.

It is clear that the cat family possesses a complex vocabulary of social signs, which the experts are gradually beginning to understand. Animals of the same species can communicate with each other by modulating the voice and by the intensity of the purring sound they make. They also communicate by means of their odorous secretions—quite obviously incomprehensible to man—which result from a particular state of mind in the animal or a given physiological situation.

A whole range of efficient visual signals also exists, easily understood, not only by the expert, but also by the trainer, or by owners of cats who are usually able to recognize the different moods of their animals. Twitching of the tail, for example, is usually a clear indication of excitement. The freely mobile ear-flaps are yet another excellent means of communication, all the more so as they usually present different colour patterns externally and internally: very light on the inside and darker outside, sometimes with specific marks which serve to identify the species. In his studies of the behaviour of the cat, Leyhausen

specially scented urine, and at these boundaries, when rivals confront each other, their tendencies to attack or retreat are equally balanced. It is probable that in most species of the cat family the individuals lead solitary lives, both males and females defending their own territories.

Territorial conflict does not normally end in a bloody struggle. Since the intruder is placed in a less advantageous position, all the defender has to do is to adopt a threatening posture. The animal will raise the hair on its back, open its jaws as wide as possible, dilate the pupils and

Right: As soon as the cubs begin to walk the lioness rejoins the pride. The lion is very patient with his offspring, and in this respect is most unusual among the male cats

revealed the relationship between the position of the ear-flaps and the cat's state of mind. When the ear-flaps are flattened and held slightly to the back of the head the animal is calm; if, however, they are held taut and the inner surfaces face forward this implies a gradual increase in the animal's alertness. An intermediate position indicates that the animal is becoming increasingly frightened.

In species which tend to form family groups, such as the lion, aggression acts as a regulating factor in social relationships. A true hierarchy based on social rank becomes established with the most aggressive animals occupying the top rungs of the ladder. Even here the struggle for power and its subsequent maintenance becomes stereotyped with exchanges of menacing but ritualized signals. These signals merely confront each contender with an indication of the aggressive nature and the latent capabilities of its opponent. Once defined and accepted, the hierarchical order keeps the expression of aggression by individual animals within reasonable limits, and, at this point, it is enough for the higher-ranking animals in the group to approach those lower down the scale for the latter to move away without showing any sign of a reciprocal threat. The submitting animals usually give a clear indication that they are prepared to give way. Observations on the social behaviour of wild lions are scanty. Some observers report that the prides have a typical hierarchical structure, while others believe that one male dominates the rest, who, although subordinate, are equal among themselves.

Even courtship, which is the overture to mating, is strongly conditioned by the aggressive drive of the partners. At first the animals appear to act as rivals and the ritual courtship opens with a succession of reciprocal threatening signals. However, for a female in breeding condition these do not last long and, as previously described, she crouches and offers the nape of her neck to the male as a signal that she is ready for mating.

Bruce Coleman/N. Myers

Left. A leopard has seized its victim and drags it away to begin his meal

Right: The cheetah may expend a great deal of energy in capturing its prey, and will tenaciously defend it against any marauding intruder

The species of the cat family

In this chapter basic facts such as size, general appearance and distribution are given for the individual species of the cat family, together with the more salient points about their behaviour, including reproduction. Unfortunately, it is not possible to present exactly the same information for each species, as not all the cats have been studied in the same depth. Obviously, most information is known about those animals whose behaviour can be closely observed, and these, of course, are usually those which have been kept in captivity.

The lion
Panthera leo

Height to shoulder: 95–110 cm (male)
Length without tail: 225–285 cm
Length of tail: 75–90 cm
Weight: 125–225 kg

It is almost superfluous to describe this species in detail, as it is the best known of the cat family. We will therefore confine ourselves to the most important features of its appearance.

Right: A cheetah (Acinonyx jubatus) in all its enigmatic elegance

Below: The majestic appearance of the male lion (Panthera leo) is accentuated by the abundant mane which is at its most luxuriant when the animal is about five years old

It is the only member of the cat family which presents distinct sexual dimorphism. The male is larger than the female, and has a massive head with a magnificent mane which is fully grown at the age of four to five years. The mane provides a striking contrast to the very short coat of the trunk. The large fan of long hair descends from the neck and shoulders, although with extreme variations of size and colour between the different lion populations. It may even vary from animal to animal within the same pride.

Both male and female have a very long tail which—uniquely in the cat family—ends in a prominent tuft of hair.

The pelage is basically grey to dark brown, only slightly marked in the adult, but spotted in the young.

Distribution: Lives in the African savanna. In Asia it is limited to the Forest of Gir in Kathiawar, India.

Behaviour: It has a wide range of prey, always large sized beasts. However, it prefers antelopes, impalas, zebras, gnus, buffaloes and warthogs, which it hunts by sight (as opposed to smell), felling the animal with one blow from its paw.

Reproduction: Gestation 105–112 days; producing two to four and sometimes up to six cubs, which are mature at the age of three or four years.

The cheetah
Acinonyx jubatus

Height to shoulder: 70–80 cm
Length without tail: 120 cm
Length of tail: 65 cm
Weight: 42–65 kg

With its sleek and extremely elegant body, the cheetah is quite unmistakeable. The back is curved at the level of the shoulders and the legs are very long and lean. The claws are non-retractile in the adult animal. The rounded head is small. The young have small manes, covering the dorsal region from the neck to the shoulders.

The tawny-coloured coat is marked with almost round, black spots which are distributed uniformly over the whole body. The first part of the tail is also spotted, but the end of the tail is ringed. The underside of the body is almost white.

A distinguishing characteristic of the cheetah is the two black bands, running down from the eyes to the angle of the mouth, which give the animal its typically melancholy expression.

Formerly, unusual blotched specimens from Rhodesia were erroneously regarded as a completely separate species (*A. rex*), but are now

Ardea Photographics / M. D. England

known to be aberrant individuals of the normal cheetah species already described. These 'king cheetahs' have dark and very irregular stripes on the coat, running longitudinally across the back and transversely over the flanks.

The coat of the young cheetah differs in colouring from that of the adults. It is greyish in colour and the spots are at first barely distinguishable.
Distribution: Found on the African savanna and Asiatic plains.
Behaviour: This is usually a solitary animal, although it may sometimes live in small groups. It is usually active in the daytime, especially during the cooler morning and evening hours, although occasionally it hunts by moonlight. It throws itself on its prey in flight, hurling it to the ground and killing it with the teeth. The only sharp claw is that on the digit corresponding to the human thumb, which does not come into contact with the ground and is therefore not blunted.

Normally the cheetah is a silent animal: it has a quiet cry like a subdued chattering but, when angry, it makes a noise more like the snarling of a dog. The cheetah purrs like all the cats, with the characteristic r'rr, r'rr sound.
Reproduction: Gestation 95 days; producing two to four cubs.

The leopard or panther
Panthera pardus

Height to shoulder: 70 cm
Length without tail: 125–150 cm
Length of tail: 90 cm
Weight: 50–80 kg

This is a large, elegant, but robust animal, possessing a short, thick, soft coat of a tawny yellow shade. The large spots are uniformly distributed on the back and flanks with the typical rosette appearance, paler in the centre. The long, strong tail is also spotted. Almost completely black (melanistic) animals occur.

Because it is distributed over such a vast area (Africa and Asia), and adapts to such a range of environments, there are considerable variations in appearance.
Behaviour: The leopard is an excellent climber, often spending the day resting on the branch of a tree. It is a nocturnal animal, mainly hunting small antelopes and gazelles, warthogs, hyraxes, baboons, rodents and birds.

Generally solitary in habit, it only associates with others of its kind at the time of mating.
Reproduction: Gestation about 92 days; usually producing two to three cubs.

Below: The extinction of the leopard (Panthera pardus), which has been wiped out in much of its former range, can only be averted by active protection of the animal and by banning the sale of its highly prized coat

Right: The African wild cat (Felis libyca) *is probably the progenitor of the present day domestic cat*

The African wild cat
Felis libyca

As big as, or slightly larger than, the domestic cat. Maximum length of tail equal to that of the domestic cat.

The pelage colour varies from individual to individual. In some, the back and flanks tend to grey, in others to rather dark beige or an ochre shade. All the intermediate shades between the above colours can be found. Vertical stripes, or lines of spots, appear on the coat, but all are pale and rather ill-defined. The end of the tail and the lower parts of the legs are clearly marked with a more pronounced pattern of bands. The underside, and the inner side of the legs are of a much lighter shade. The largish ears tend to be a reddish shade on the outer surfaces.

Distribution: Lives mainly on the African savanna.

Behaviour: A carnivorous animal, nocturnal in habit. It eats lizards, snakes, hares, rodents in general, and small antelopes, and will eat insects and fruit if necessary. The voice is a raucous miaowing.

Reproduction: 56 days gestation. Two to five young are born, which the mother hides in natural holes, usually between boulders.

The serval or African leopard cat
Felis serval

Height to shoulder: 55 cm
Length without tail: 70 cm
Length of tail: 30 cm
Weight: 14–18 kg

The serval has a slender body with a proportionally smaller head. Its well-developed ears appear oval when extended.

The ground colour is brownish-yellow on the back and flanks, much paler or whitish on the underside. A series of dark brown stripes begins at the neck and opens out over the back and down to the flanks, ending in a more or less regular linear pattern of spots. The tail is ringed.

A variety known as the servalina is found in the western regions of Africa, where it can co-exist with the true serval. It is distinguished from the latter mainly by its colouring. This tends to grey and presents a diffuse and attenuated spotted pattern, rather than stripes.

Distribution: Found all over Africa with the exception of the Sahara and the extreme south of the continent.

Behaviour: Although mainly nocturnal, the serval does sometimes feed during the day. It may hunt the same small game as *F. libyca*, but because of

its larger size and speed in running over short distances, it can more easily tackle small antelopes such as duikers, which are its usual prey.
Reproduction: Gestation lasts about 70 days. The female gives birth to two to four young which are taken care of in any lair that can be found—small caves, tree cavities or even abandoned termite nests.

The caracal or African lynx
Felis caracal

Height to shoulder: 45 cm
Length without tail: 75 cm
Length of tail: 25 cm
Weight: 15–18 kg

This species is related to the European and American lynx, and has the same tuft of stiff hair at the ear tips. The tail is very short, shorter than in all other African cats, while the hind legs are obviously much longer than the forelegs. The head is flattened frontally and has long, narrow, tipped ear-flaps. The outer surfaces of the ear-flaps are blackish in colour. The coat is almost completely tawny on the flanks, with whitish fur, lightly spotted, on the underside. Two characteristic dark stripes extend from the inner angles of the eyes to the nostrils.
Distribution: From the east of the African continent through Arabia as far as India.
Behaviour: Feeds mainly at night, hunting small antelopes, rodents, hyraxes, and birds which it often catches in flight. It sometimes attacks domestic fowls and lambs.
Reproduction: The female gives birth to two to five young, which very soon take on an adult appearance, apart from the colouring which is lighter, tending to grey.

The South African black-footed cat
Felis nigripes

Rather thick-set and smaller than the domestic cat.
Height to shoulder: 25 cm

This animal has a relatively large head with rounded ear-flaps, and a rather short, thick tail. The coat is of long, soft fur, and is a brownish-yellow colour on the back and flanks, and very light, sometimes completely white, on the underside. There is a distinct pattern of black spots fanning out from the shoulders and running over the back and flanks. The tail is incompletely

ringed in black, and black-tipped. The lower parts of the legs are striped. A distinguishing characteristic is the black colour of those parts of the paws which come into contact with the ground.

Distribution: Found only in southern Africa.

Behaviour: Little is known of the behaviour of this cat, as it is not common.

The African golden cat
Felis aurata

A large cat slightly bigger than the serval, but heavier and with a longer tail.

The ear-flaps on the squat head are short, with rounded rims and black markings. The shape of the ears, together with the tail length, distinguishes this cat from the serval, and because of the difference in colour there is little possibility of confusion.

It is short-haired and usually golden brown on the back and flanks, becoming lighter towards the underside which is white. In a number of individuals the ground colour tends to deeper grey. Only in the latter specimens does the dark spotting, which is more evident, cover the whole body. In the golden cat proper, the dark brown spotting is clearly defined on the ventral surfaces only.

Distribution: It has a limited distribution in the equatorial forests of Africa.

Behaviour: It lives mainly on rodents and hyraxes, as well as birds.

Left: The serval's preferred prey is birds which it is extremely skilful at catching. Domestic fowls, unfortunately, present an irresistible attraction to it and it may wreak havoc in the farmyard

Above right: Caracal, or African lynx (Felis caracal)

Ardea Photographics/K. W. Fink

Right: Black-footed cat (Felis nigripes). *This small cat, studied in captivity by Leyhausen, is a very poor jumper and a rather reluctant climber*

Jacana/J. X. Sundance

The sand cat
Felis margarita

Somewhat smaller than the domestic cat.

This animal has long, soft, thick hair, very light, tending to beige or pale grey, and a little paler on the underside. Some slightly darker stripes appear on the back and flanks, and there are two dark bands on the lower legs. It has a ringed, long-haired tail of medium length, tipped in black.

Because of the relatively long hair, the almost white head seems bigger than it really is. Brown stripes extend vertically from between the ears to the eyes. The large, triangular shaped ear-flaps are placed towards the sides of the head.

Distribution: Fringes of the Sahara desert and desert regions of Arabia and Turkestan.

Behaviour: Hunts primarily rodents and birds.

Reproduction: The young (about four at each birth) are more prominently spotted than the adults.

The fishing cat
Felis viverrina

Height to shoulder: 38 cm
Length without tail: 70–75 cm
Tail length: 30 cm
Weight: 11–14 kg

This animal looks like a large domestic cat. The hair is rough and short on the back and flanks, longer and shaggier on the underside.

The dull coat, which is basically greyish-yellow and crossed with very irregular longitudinal black spots, is of no particular economic

Left: The sand cat (Felis margarita) has an almost uniformly coloured coat, giving the animal a better chance of concealment in its arid surroundings. The paws and tail are striped

Above: The fishing cat (Felis viverrina) is, even in infancy, a savage animal, and the adult develops the physical strength to become a formidable predator

Right: The jungle cat (Felis chaus) is quite closely related to the European wild cat, and inhabits very thick bush country, swampy forests and impenetrable reed-beds. The tail is rather short, and the ear sometimes bear small tufts, suggesting some affinity with the lynxes

value. Transverse stripes can be seen on the lower legs, and the tail has about eight or nine ill-defined ring markings. There are three to five fairly thin stripes clearly visible on the forehead, running from the eyes to the nape of the neck; these lateral stripes really consist of many small, closely grouped spots.

The eyes, with rounded, as opposed to elliptical pupils, are of a characteristic bronze colour.
Distribution: Found in India, Ceylon, Nepal, Java, Sumatra and Indo-China, the fishing cat lives in wooded areas along water courses, principally in marshy districts.
Behaviour: For its size it is very fierce, and has been known to tackle large prey such as goats. Usually, however, it hunts smaller mammals and birds. Whether it eats fish, as implied by its English name which is an accurate translation of its Bengali name, is open to doubt.
Reproduction: Gestation about 63 days; litter usually one to four young.

The jungle cat
Felis chaus

Height to shoulder: 40 cm
Length without tail: 60 cm
Length of tail: 30 cm
Weight: 5–6 kg

In some of its habitats, particularly in Africa, this animal could be confused with the wild African cat (*Felis libyca*), for from the Nile Valley to India the ranges of the two species overlap. However, it is a bigger animal and it can also be differentiated from *Felis libyca* by the relatively short tail and the barely perceptible coat pattern.

The basic colour tends to a tawny shade, with smoky reddish-brown on the back, and beige on the underside. The head is lighter in colour than the rest of the body, and the narrow, pricked ear-flaps are brownish-red on the outer surfaces. Small tufts of hair appear on the tips of the ear-flaps, but they are not so prominent as in the lynx.

Only the tip of the black, spotted tail is ringed. Indistinct brown spots and bands may appear on the flanks and lower legs.
Distribution: The jungle cat is found mainly in the Asian continent, where it prefers to live in marshy reed bed areas, usually very well watered. It is distributed in Asia from the Caucasus and Turkestan to India and the Indo-Chinese peninsula. It is also found in Africa but is mainly limited to the Nile Delta.

41

The tiger

Panthera tigris

Height to shoulder: about 100 cm
Length without tail: 200–280 cm
Length of tail: about 100 cm
Weight: 200–270 kg

This animal is agile and elegant but at the same time, extraordinarily powerful. The fur is short and lustrous, except on the cheeks which have whitish whiskers. The ground colour of the coat is usually a golden yellow, with brown shading on the back. The underside, the inner surfaces of the legs, the tip of the muzzle, the cheeks and the chest are all white. Black transverse stripes, sometimes doubled or simply divided at the ends, extend from the back, slightly obliquely, towards the underside. The forehead, cheeks and legs are also striped, and the tail is clearly ringed but without any tuft of hair. As the animal has a very extensive geographical distribution over a large part of Asia, from latitude 8 degrees South to latitude 55 degrees North, the ground colour of

43

the coat varies and may be a more or less dark shade; the darker specimens are usually found among forest tigers.

Melanistic individuals are also seen, as well as the partially albino type with paler bands. The depth of colour of the bands may also vary slightly from population to population.

The tiger's rounded head is very large with circular, rimmed ear-flaps. The legs are powerful and the tail is large. The females are a little smaller than the males.

Distribution: This animal is widely distributed over the Asian continent from the Caucasus mountains and Iran to China and Southern Mongolia, and from India to Malaysia, Java and Bali.

Behaviour: The tiger is a cunning, fierce animal which preys on most mammals, except the larger kinds such as adult elephants. It will also feed on birds, fish, tortoises or lizards. Some tigers haunt villages and attack domestic cattle and sheep. The man-eating tiger is however very rare; they are nearly always either females trying to feed their young when food is scarce, or older, enfeebled animals.

The sound most often made by the tiger is a deep, guttural growling. In attacking it sometimes lets out a sharp, insistently repeated shriek and it snarls when intimidated.

Reproduction: The tiger is a solitary animal; males and females associate only in the mating season. In the north, coupling takes place three months after the thaw has set in; elsewhere it may occur at any time of the year. Gestation lasts about 105 days and the litter consists of two to six cubs. They are as big as the fully-grown domestic cat, and are born with their eyes closed.

The ocelot or American leopard cat
Felis pardalis

Height to shoulder: 50 cm
Length without tail: up to 100 cm
Length of tail: 40–45 cm
Weight: 16 kg

The ocelot is easily distinguishable by its size together with the pattern of the coat and the soft, short hair. The basic colour is very light, tending to ash-yellow or brownish-yellow. A series of longitudinal black stripes start from the neck and run over the back and flanks. In some inidividuals these join in pairs to form elongated elliptical patterns, which fade to grey-brown towards the centre. The markings are particularly evident on the forepart of the trunk. At the rump they continue in a series of complete black spots or in longitudinal lines of dark, but often incompletely closed, ring-like markings. On the forehead, thin lines cross longitudinally; the cheeks are transversely crossed. Black spots appear on the under side, legs and tail.

There are many variations of the pattern which has been briefly described. The females have a rather paler pattern, also recognizable by the plain spotting which is rounded in the hip and shoulder regions. The fur is much prized.

Distribution: The southern regions of North America, Mexico, Central America (excluding the West Indies) and a large part of South America.

Behaviour: The ocelot lives a solitary life. It usually hunts at night although it may sometimes hunt in the morning and at dusk. An excellent

Bruce Coleman / H. Schultz

tree climber, it is an expert at catching birds, and will also eat small mammals, including young monkeys. It is normally afraid of man.

The adult spits when afraid or angry, murmurs when satisfied and miaows when ill.

Reproduction: Mating from October to January. Gestation about 70 days, with the litters consisting of two or more young.

Above: This young ocelot, like all kittens, is full of curiosity and is searching for interesting 'prey' in the hole of an old tree-trunk

The margay
Felis wiedi

Length without tail: 61 cm
Length of tail: 40 cm
Weight: 6 kg

Although a little smaller in size, this animal is very similar to the ocelot, so much so that it is

Marka

Right: For some unknown reason the ocelot (Felis pardalis) does not appear on the list of animals whose skins it is prohibited to sell. It is now literally disappearing from its habitat, where, up to a few years ago, it was still fairly numerous

far from easy to distinguish the coat pattern of one from the other. However, the margay's rounded head is proportionally smaller; it has dark brown eyes, and the white-tufted black tail is relatively longer.

Distribution: A little known animal, inhabiting American forests from the southern United States to the Argentine.

Behaviour: It is an exceptional climber and can descend from trees with great speed, jump in a truly acrobatic fashion from tree to tree, and run up and down the waving branches of climbing plants.

It is thought that the margay mainly hunts birds and small arboreal mammals.

Reproduction: Gestation about 70 days. One or two young usually make up a litter, although there are sometimes more. They are darker in colour than the adults.

The tiger cat or tigrillo
Felis tigrina

Length without tail: 60 cm
Length of tail: 45 cm

The tiger cat is very similar to the margay but not so big and with a smaller and longer head. The eyes, with bright irises, are also small, and the coat is not so smooth.

Distribution: American tropical forests.

Behaviour: It is an excellent climber, living in forests and normally feeding on birds and small mammals, although it will also eat lizards and big insects.

Reproduction: Gestation lasts about 75 days, following which one or two young, or occasionally more, are born with their eyes closed. They begin to feed independently after two months.

The pampas cat or colocolo
Felis colocolo

Length without tail: 76 cm
Length of tail: 25 cm

The pampas cat is easily recognizable, being the only South American cat with ears which are pointed, not rounded. The eyes are brownish-yellow, with vertical pupils. The coat varies considerably. It usually has a silver or ochre-grey background, indistinctly marked with elongated or ringed spots, in reddish-brown or grey, while the lower parts of the body and inner sides of the paws are black. The long hair on the back sticks out, and, when the animal is excited, takes on the appearance of a small mane.

Distribution: The pampas cats are widely distributed in South America, the ideal habitat being a wooded plateau or the pampas itself.

Behaviour: Little is known of their behaviour, but it is thought that they feed on small rodents, birds and also small reptiles, and are mainly terrestrial in habit.

Geoffroy's cat
Felis geoffroyi

Length without tail: 60 cm
Length of tail: 35 cm

The coat varies from yellow to a pearly greyish-brown, with spotting similar to that of the margay.

Distribution: Found in the southern regions of the South American continent, from Bolivia to Patagonia.

Behaviour: This animal lives in rocky and bushy areas and sleeps in trees. It hunts birds and small mammals, and is a very good climber and swimmer.

Reproduction: The female bears two or three young each year, keeping them hidden in rock holes or between bushes.

The kodkod
Felis guigna

Length without tail: 45 cm
Length of tail: 22 cm

This animal has a somewhat squat body with small paws and a coat very similar to that of Geoffroy's cat, but with slightly smaller spots. Almost completely black, or melanistic, individuals have been observed. The claws are very strong.

Distribution: Inhabits the wooded and bushy areas of Chile and Bolivia, and the Andean foothills.

Behaviour: Little is known of the behaviour of this animal in the wild, although it is thought that it is terrestrial in habit. It usually hunts small mammals.

Bruce Coleman/F. Erize

Left: The coat of the pampas cat (Felis colocolo) *varies considerably, depending on the particular area in which it lives. This has resulted in the division of the species into numerous varieties*

*Above: A beautiful
specimen of a jaguar
(Panthera onca). The
pattern of the coat is
clearly visible, and
the characteristic
spotting in the centre
of the rosettes
distinguishes the coat
from that of the leopard*

The Andean cat
Felis jacobita

Length without tail: 80 cm
Length of tail: 50 cm

The Andean cat or mountain cat has a thick, soft, silver-grey coat, tending to white under the body and to an ashen shade on the back. It has a pattern of yellowish spots and rings, merging into rounded black spots on the abdomen and paws.
Distribution: Lives in the Andes mountain chain at heights of up to 5,000 m (15,000 feet).

The jaguar
Panthera onca

Height to shoulder: 70 cm
Length without tail: 150–180 cm
Length of tail: 60–70 cm
Weight: 70–130 kg

This animal is remarkable for its strength, mas-sive appearance and ponderous gait. It is the only representative of the genus *Panthera* in the American continent.

The short but very soft coat is basically fawn in colour, with lighter patches on the underside and the tip of the muzzle. The pattern is quite characteristic: numerous clear black spots on the head and lower parts of the legs, with the remainder of the body thickly covered with large rosettes in the form of irregular, polygonal black rings with lighter centres. There are a few dark spots in the centres of most of the rosettes. On the back the spots join to form a dark longitudi-nal band, following the vertebral column almost down to the tail.
Distribution: Tropical forests of Central and South America.
Behaviour: The jaguar is a typical forest cat, preferring humid areas along water courses or the edges of marshy zones. In spite of its large size, it sometimes climbs trees and it is also a good swimmer. It usually hunts at dawn or sunset, or during the night when there is a full moon.

Left: The jaguar
(Panthera onca) *is a*
marvellously equipped
and fearless predator.
It sometimes succeeds in
killing the large marine
turtles which gather
on beaches to lay their
eggs

Okapia

Bruce Coleman / L. R. Dawson

*Above: European lynx
(Felis lynx lynx).
Above right: The
slightly smaller lynx of
the Iberian peninsula
(Felis lynx pardellus).
The Spanish lynx has a
shorter coat with a more
prominent pattern than
the northern subspecies*

It will usually eat any of the larger American vertebrates, including capybaras, tapirs and deer.

It is a solitary animal and the male only associates with the female during the mating season (August–September).

Reproduction: Gestation about 90 days; litter, two or three cubs.

The common European lynx
Felis lynx lynx

Height to shoulder: 60–75 cm
Length without tail: 80–130 cm
Length of tail: 11–24 cm
Weight: 18–20 kg

The common lynx can be easily distinguished from the wild cat (*F. silvestris*) by its longer legs, very short tail, tufts of black hair (about 3 cm long) on the tips of the ear-flaps, and the large black and white whiskers framing the muzzle. The typical European form is usually regarded as a subspecies of a species which also includes the Spanish lynx and the Canadian lynx.

The dominant colour of the coat is brown, but it is rich in reddish and grey shading. The underside is basically a very light ash-grey. Darker stripes cover the back and the paws, while the tail is ringed, black-tipped and white on the under surface.

Varieties with a uniform, fawnish-yellow coat with no distinctive pattern also occur. In winter the coat colour becomes paler and the fur adapts to suit the climate—although it is still long and soft during the other seasons of the year.

Distribution: Scandinavia, Poland and Siberia.

Behaviour: The lynx is a typical forest predator, but is everywhere on the decline. It usually hunts during the day, its prey being chamois, hares, marmots, badgers, pheasants, woodcocks, partridges, mice and small birds. When discovered, it stands quite still, and stares fixedly at the hunter.

Reproduction: Mates in January and February without any long courtship. Gestation lasts about 70 days, the litter usually consisting of two or three young, born with their eyes closed.

The Spanish lynx
Felis lynx pardellus

Height to shoulder: 60–70 cm
Length without tail: 85–110 cm
Length of tail: 12.5–13 cm
Weight: 15–20 kg

This animal is slightly smaller than the very closely related common European lynx, and, like the latter, has pricked ears with tufts of black hair, and long whiskers. The deep colour of the coat is a distinguishing characteristic of this animal. The light shade is confined to the underside, while the back and flanks are brown with reddish shading, and covered with black stripes and small, rounded spots. The stripes, which are longitudinal on the neck and back, run

49

transversely over the flanks. The pattern varies widely between individuals. Some have predominant stripes, others small close spotting, while between these two extremes there is a whole range of intermediate combinations.

The tail is smaller than that of the European lynx and is spotted, except for the tip which is completely black.

Distribution: This is a rare animal, once inhabiting the mountain forests and mountain slopes of southern Europe, but now surviving only in Spain.

Behaviour: It is a twilight and nocturnal animal and, like the common European lynx, ambushes its prey. It can climb trees although not to a great height, and is an exceptionally good jumper and swimmer. It is a solitary animal and male and female only associate during the mating season.

The animal emits a kind of shrill spitting sound. During the courtship a screeching miaow, changing to a deep bass sound, is uttered.

Reproduction: Similar to the common European lynx.

Above: The bobcat (Felis rufa) usually makes its lair between rocks or in caves, carefully lining it with dried leaves, brushwood and moss

Left: The paws of the European lynx provide a good example of this animal's adaptation to its habitat. They are large in relation to the cat's size and are covered with long thick fur. This makes it easier for the lynx to move through the snow and affords protection against the cold

The Canadian lynx
Felis lynx canadensis

Height to shoulder: 50–60 cm
Length without tail: 70–100 cm
Length of tail: 10–15 cm

Some experts regard this as a separate species, but it is very similar to the lynxes of Europe and northern Asia, and is here treated as a subspecies.

The silver-grey fur, with its reddish-brown shading and vaguely defined spotted pattern, is highly prized. The hair is longer on the flanks and lower legs. A series of quite clearly defined longitudinal black stripes appear on the forehead, and white whiskers are present on the muzzle. The striped tail is short and tipped with black.

The Canadian lynx can be distinguished from the European lynx by the length of the hair (especially on the flanks), which gives the coat an extremely soft appearance, and by its overall colour, which is grey. The long and luxuriant whiskers, together with the muzzle hair, give the head an unusually massive appearance.

Distribution: Canada and the northern United States.

Behaviour: A typical animal of the North American forest, it is active mainly at twilight and by night, hiding during the day in a tree cavity, on a low branch or in a bush. It usually preys on rabbits or hares, but it will eat other small mammals and birds.

Reproduction: Similar to the common European lynx.

The bobcat or red lynx
Felis rufa

Length without tail: 75 cm
Length of tail: 15 cm
Weight: 10–12 kg

The bobcat is smaller than the Canadian lynx and can be distinguished from the latter animal by its fur, which is luxuriant, although not long, and mainly reddish-brown in colour. The basic, spotted pattern of the coat is clearly visible with small black spots covering the whole body. Dark, transverse stripes appear on the lower legs, although they are not particularly distinct.

Distribution: Occurs in some numbers in most of the United States, particularly in California. It inhabits rough open country, frequenting thickets and scrub, hiding among rocks where vegetation is sparse.

Behaviour: Like all the lynxes, this animal stays hidden during the day and becomes active at twilight, preying upon rabbits, hares, squirrels and mice. It does not normally attack man and usually keeps well away from dwelling places. It may, however, approach them when it is feeding its young, and its usual prey is scarce.

Reproduction: Gestation 50–60 days. Birth takes place in spring when two to four young are born.

The European wild cat
Felis silvestris

Height to shoulder: 35–40 cm
Length without tail: 50 cm
Length of tail: 30 cm
Weight: 6–8 kg

This animal is slightly smaller than the domestic

Below: The beautiful European wild cat can display great cunning, though it is cautious by nature

Marka

cat. It has a sturdier body with a larger head and a clubbed, round-ended tail with seven to nine clearly defined black rings. The whole of the body is covered with luxuriant hair. The basic coat colour is yellowish-grey with dark grey stripes crossing the flanks from the back to the lower legs. The underside is lighter with a prominent, large, whitish patch covering the throat. The insides of the ear-flaps and the tip of the muzzle are also white. Five clearly defined, black lines extend from the eyebrows longitudinally across the forehead, merging into the hair at neck level. A well marked, dark band runs along the whole spine down to the base of the tail. The gaze is very penetrating.

Distribution: Can still be found in remote areas including the Scottish highlands.

Behaviour: A typical cat of the broadleaved and coniferous forests, it is suspicious of man, and hunts at night and at twilight by lying in wait for its victims, making full use of its protective colouring to conceal itself. It preys on small carnivores, young deer, hares, marmots, squirrels, mice and birds. When near water courses or small lakes it will catch fish, and it is very skilful at catching aquatic birds. It does not go higher than 1,800 m (5,500 feet) above sea level. It is a solitary animal and male and female only associate during the mating season (around February).

Reproduction: Couples after a long period of excruciating miaowing and yowling, in the same way as the domestic cat. Gestation lasts 62 days and the litter consists of up to six kittens.

The puma, cougar or mountain lion
Felis concolor

Height to shoulder: 65 cm
Length without tail: 150 cm
Length of tail: 90 cm
Weight: 120 kg

The puma has a rather rounded head and tough, short, circular ear-flaps. The thick, short-haired coat is basically a uniformly reddish-brown colour, dark on the back and flanks, but lighter on the underside, the throat and the inner surfaces of the legs. The tip of the muzzle has a characteristically near-white area round the mouth, which is encircled by a very dark stripe running from the nostrils to the corners of the mouth itself.

The young puma can be immediately identified from the adult by the distinct dark spots on a fawn ground, and also by the ringed tail. When the animal is 70–80 days old the coat assumes its adult pattern.

Above: A puma (Felis concolor) in its natural environment

Right: A close-up of the head of a puma. The dividing line between the edge of the mucous membrane of the nose and the fur-covered skin can be clearly seen. The line has the characteristic curve common to all species of the genus Felis

Left: Zoologically, the clouded leopard (Panthera nebulosa) can be regarded as a link between the genera Panthera *and* Felis. *It shares with the first genus an identical cranial structure and dentition, and with the second a number of morphological characteristics. These include the typical resting position in which the paws are folded at the carpal joint and tucked under the chest. For these reasons the clouded leopard is sometimes placed alone in the genus* Neofelis

Distribution: Extends over almost the whole of the American continent from Canada to Patagonia, except where killed off by man. It is at home in any environment from the plains to the mountain regions.

Behaviour: A good tree climber and an excellent hunter, it preys on mammals, primarily deer. In the attack, it tears its victim's throat open and greedily drinks the warm blood. It lives alone and associates in pairs only during the mating season.

It does not roar, but emits a shrill howling noise, beginning on a high note and dropping to a much quieter sound. It also purrs.

Reproduction: Gestation 90 days. There are usually two to three young in a litter but there can be up to six.

The clouded leopard or clouded panther
Panthera nebulosa

Height to shoulder: 40 cm
Length without tail: 105–110 cm
Tail length: 70–90 cm
Weight: 18–20 kg

This animal has a graceful and slender body with rather short, robust legs. The tail is long and thick. These are the essential distinguishing characteristics of the clouded leopard, although it is easily recognized by its almost uniquely spotted coat.

The skin is very highly prized, not only for the intrinsic beauty of its patterns, but because of the animal's rarity. The coat is greyish-beige, the colour varying in depth from individual to individual. The ground colour has a pattern of numerous brown spots differing in size, with the dark polygonal-shaped outlines becoming lighter towards the centre.

The name 'clouded' is in fact derived from this coat pattern. The legs and tail, however, are covered with relatively smaller and uniformly dark spots. Small, elliptically grouped spots appear on the forehead. Another characteristic marking is the slender stripe which extends from the outer angle of the eyes and crosses over the whole temporal region.

Distribution: Lives in the region to the south-east of the Himalayas as far as Indonesia. It moves up to higher levels, but not usually above altitudes of 3,000 m (9,000 feet).

Behaviour: The clouded leopard is a solitary animal. An accomplished climber, it spends most of the day in trees where it catches birds with great agility. These comprise the major part of its diet, but it also eats small mammals.

The snow leopard or ounce
Panthera uncia

Height to shoulder: 60 cm
Length without tail: up to 130 cm
Length of tail: up to 100 cm
Weight: 30–40 kg

This animal is typical of the mountain regions of central Asia. It is easily distinguished from the leopard by its smaller size, thicker and longer fur, and lighter colour. It has a massive head with a rather short muzzle and relatively small, rounded ear-flaps.

The basic colour tends to cream or light grey-brown, being lighter on the underside. The pattern is more or less easy to identify, depending on the season. In winter, for example, when the fur is rather long, the spots are somewhat blurred. Small, black spots are dotted over the head while the back, flanks, and upper surfaces of the tail are covered with rosettes similar to those of the leopard but less well defined.

Distribution: Himalayas and Altai mountains.

Behaviour: Little is known of the snow leopard's behaviour because of the difficulty in observing the animal in its natural habitat. It is probably solitary and, at most, forms small family groups occupying a vast territory. It is nocturnal, resting during the day in a rock cavity, and often choosing a cave as a permanent home. This den is easy to locate as eventually a thick carpet of tufts of hair shed by the animals builds up outside the entrance. It hunts herbivores such as wild goats on the mountain heights.

Reproduction: Mates in winter. The gestation period is 93–99 days; birth occurs in spring when the number of cubs in the litter is usually between two and four.

The marbled cat
Felis marmorata

Length without tail: 45 cm
Length of tail: 45 cm

A small and quite rare cat very similar to the clouded leopard in appearance, but considerably smaller in size. The stripes on the cheeks are clearly defined, while those on the flanks are clouded. The legs, tail and lower parts of the body present a much finer spotting. The pupils of the large, brown eyes are slit-like.

Below: Little is known of the habits of the snow leopard (Panthera uncia). *It lives in the high mountains and each individual roams over a vast hunting territory, living a completely solitary existence, apart from the brief period of courtship*

Distribution: Lives in the forests of southern Asia from the Himalayas to Sumatra and Borneo.
Behaviour: Preys on small rodents and birds.

The Asian leopard or Bengal cat
Felis bengalensis

Length without tail: up to 60 cm
Length of tail: 40 cm
Weight: 3–4 kg

The coat varies from ochre to light brown among populations living in the south of the range of distribution, and is silver-grey among those in the north. Black spotting sometimes extends as far as the abdomen and inside surfaces of the legs, which are normally white. The eyes are brownish or greenish-yellow.
Distribution: These animals avoid the arid regions. They are found in the wooded areas of the Amur river, Manchuria, China and Indo-China, and in Malaya, Borneo and the Philippines. They move up to altitudes of 3,000 m (9,000 feet).
Behaviour: The leopard cats are primarily twilight and night hunters, mostly preying on small animals such as rats, mice, squirrels, and sometimes hares and fowls when nothing better can be found.
Reproduction: Little is known of the mating habits, but it has been observed that gestation lasts about 56 days and the litter usually consists of two to four young. The reproductive period, it seems, is not linked to any particular season.

The rusty-spotted or red cat
Felis rubiginosa

This small cat has a brownish-grey coat with reddish stripes running over the neck and shoulders and ending in spots on the back and flanks. It is closely related to the Asian leopard cat and very similar in appearance, but smaller in size.
Distribution: It lives in the dry regions of southern India and Ceylon where it frequents long grass and scrub.
Behaviour: Territorial in habit, it scratches trees to define its territory.
Reproduction: The kittens are born only in spring.

The bay cat of Borneo
Felis badia

Little is known of this species, which is found only in Borneo. It is a rather small cat, only slightly larger than the domestic cat, with a small rounded head and a uniformly reddish-coloured coat, with faint stripes on the face.

Pallas's cat
Felis manul

Pallas's cat has a heavy body with a thick, long-haired coat, smoky reddish-ochre in colour, with the shading verging on silver or black. Only the head and underside are spotted. It is about the size of a domestic cat.

Below left: Pallas's cat (Felis manul)

Below: Bengal cat or Asian leopard cat (Felis bengalensis)

Okapia

Jacana / J. X. Sundance

Distribution: On the eastern banks of the Caspian Sea, in Tibet, Mongolia and western China.
Behaviour: Partridges, voles, mice and other small rodents are its normal prey.

The jaguarundi
Felis yagouaroundi

Height to shoulder: 30–35 cm
Length without tail: 55–80 cm
Length of tail: 40 cm
Weight: 10 kg

The jaguarundi, which today is far from being a common animal, can be recognized by its characteristically dark, very soft, uniformly coloured coat, and slim, elegant silhouette. When individual hairs are examined, the roots appear lighter than the dark brown, almost black, tips. This explains the fact that when the animal is resting and the pelage is relaxed, the coat seems darker, but when afraid or irritated, the hairs bristle and appear lighter in colour.

A variety of this species, known as 'eyra', is distinguished by its chestnut-red monocoloured pelage.
Distribution: A typical cat of the forest lands, the jaguarundi extends over a part of the American continent from Mexico to Paraguay and the Argentine.
Behaviour: It is a solitary animal. It is active both by day and by night and is a good climber. It feeds on large birds, small mammals and, occasionally, fruit.

Below: Red jaguarundi (Felis yagouaroundi). This variety was previously considered to be a distinct species of the grey jaguarundi, known as the eyra

Below right: A domestic cat, the red tabby (Felis catus)

The domestic cat
Felis catus

Height to shoulder: about 30 cm
Length without tail: 40 cm
Length of tail: 25 cm
Weight: 4–8 kg

The domestic cat is usually slightly smaller in size than the European wild cat, and most easily distinguished by the outline of the end of the tail, which is pointed rather than rounded. Like most other domesticated animals, the domestic cat has been bred in a remarkable variety of colours.
Distribution: Found in all parts of the world.
Behaviour: Pampered domestic cats are capable of living very lazy lives, drinking milk or water and feeding on canned or dried pet-foods, fish, or meat. However, when necessary, domestic cats can hunt with great patience and skill. Indoors their ability to catch mice is well known. Numerous examples are known of domestic cats which have run wild and become entirely self supporting. On the whole, when left to themselves, domestic cats tend to be nocturnal, solitary and territorial in behaviour, only collecting together, sometimes in some numbers, during courtship.
Reproduction: Females can breed when they are about one year old and (unlike the female European wild cat which comes into heat only in the spring) can have two or three litters a year. Courtship is noisy. The gestation period is usually 65 or 66 days and usually there are from four to six kittens.

Jacana/A. Visage

Marka

Distribution of the best-known cats

Canadian lynx

Jaguar

Bobcat   Jaguarundi   Spanish lynx   Caracal   Clouded leopard

58

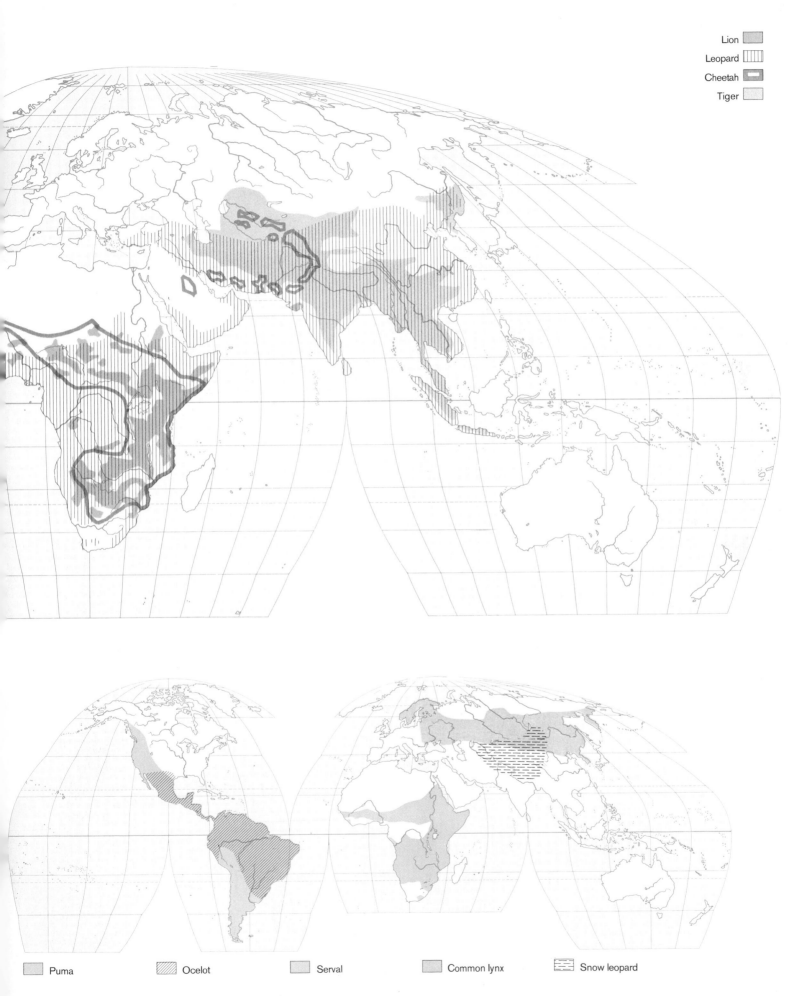

Lion
Leopard
Cheetah
Tiger

Puma   Ocelot   Serval   Common lynx   Snow leopard

59

Big cats of the savanna

When mention is made of the African savanna, even the most uninformed would probably think immediately of three cats: the lion (*Panthera leo*), the leopard (*Panthera pardus*), and the cheetah (*Acinonyx jubatus*). It is, on the whole, a rather dry and desolate environment. Regions like the savanna are present on the same latitude in a large area of South America (where it takes the name of the pampas) and in India. It is, in fact, a form of prairie in which grass is the predominating vegetation, although there may also be bushes and trees, like the African acacia, which are specially adapted to the arid nature of the soil.

The temperature is generally above 18°C (64°F), and the heat and dryness are the dominant features of the climate for the greater part of the year in the savanna areas. It is only in summer that the heavy torrential rains of the tropics come to bring life to these dusty and sunburnt stretches of land. Then, with the high temperatures mitigated by heavy rain showers, the grasses grow rapidly again, and the climatic conditions of the savanna become less extreme. During the dry season fires are very frequent, but the grasses survive relatively easily because most of them, like wild oats, have seeds which penetrate down into the earth, waiting for the first rain to arrive so that germination can once more take place. In addition, beneath the ground, the roots of many species of grasses survive unscathed to grow new leaves later.

The thin green layer on the African savanna

Left: Twilight and dusk are the best times to observe the lion, when he comes to a water hole to drink

Below: The lioness, like the domestic cat, picks up her cub by the neck in order to carry it

Marka

A lioness keeping
careful watch over her
cubs

provides the sustenance of life for an incredibly large number of herbivores, including at least 40 species of ungulates such as antelopes, gazelles, zebras, giraffes, buffaloes, and gnus, which often congregate and form large herds. The ungulates, of course, constitute prey for the predatory cats, as well as for other predators like the African wild dogs and hyaenas, and such scavengers as jackals and vultures. Thus the vegetation in the savanna converts energy from the sun and supplies both the herbivores and predators in a finely balanced cycle.

The African Lion

The African savanna lion is a subspecies called *Panthera leo leo*, and this means that it differs slightly from other populations of the *Panthera leo* species. At some time in the past the species was almost certainly a much more homogeneous and unified group than it is today. However, when a species occupies a wide area it is usually the case that different races evolve. Lions must have once occupied a continuous area much greater than the present India, Africa, Asia Minor, Greece, and Macedonia. It seems that they also occupied much of Europe in prehistoric times. Today, three subspecies remain, two in Africa and one in the Forest of Gir in India.

There must have been numerous local populations of lions differing only slightly from one another, and it seems that some of these varieties were isolated from each other and evolved separately, thus originating varied types including the subspecies which are still being studied today.

From time immemorial man has encroached on the lion's territory and, during the last few hundred years, has regarded the animal as a pest and has greatly restricted its distribution. Today the lion has completely disappeared from the Mediterranean and western coasts of Africa, and its living space in Africa is now confined to an area limited by the southern edge of the Sahara desert. The groups of lions in the most immediate danger now have to be protected in national parks.

Although all cats display some social behaviour, the lion is the only big cat which is typically gregarious in habit. It goes through its biological cycle in company with a more or less stable group of other lions. Within this group, known as the pride, there are established reproductive, hierarchical and social relationships, and occasional cooperation in the hunt. An essential point, however, is that the pride practises 'parental care', with the adult lions protecting the cubs and training them for the hunt.

Above: A pride of lions in their typical habitat

Left: The strong jaw and facial muscles of the lioness enable her to get a firm grip on a captured beast and drag it for long distances

A pride of lions usually includes at least two adult males. Morphologically the male differs from the female, being a much more massive animal. Its magnificent mane makes the huge head, which is larger that that of the female, all the more terrifying. The males are the group defenders against males of other prides. They defend the territory in which they live and from which they obtain their prey, and the extent of the area protected is determined by the richness of the prey it offers. It has been calculated that a population of at least a thousand herbivores is required for every three to four lions. This means that the area needed varies from up to 20 square miles where the ungulates are plentiful, to at least twice that area, where they are thinner on the ground.

The male lion's appearance, coupled with his terrible roar, are enough to frighten off most intruding lions who would, in any case, find themselves at a psychological disadvantage on entering another animal's territory. Fighting does not usually begin immediately an intruder appears, the defending animal limiting itself to following the enemy, roaring angrily until the latter decamps from the territory. When the defeated animal turns his back, this is usually sufficient sign for the victor to quieten down.

The male in this small society, then, has the task of defining the extent of the territory belonging to the group, in order to warn off individuals from other groups. To do this the male uses a system often practised by carnivores and known to us through the rather similar habits of the domestic dog, although in the latter species (no longer in its natural state) this particular action may now have lost much of its original significance. The lion urinates repeatedly on the ground and bushes which border its territory. The urine has a pungent and persistent smell which clings to vegetation and this acts as an olfactory warning to all rivals.

It is evident that every possible natural mechanism is built into the group to avoid direct clashes between the animals. Clearly, if such clashes did occur, tragic results to one or both of the protagonists would follow because of the lion's tremendous power and this would, of course, be a great disadvantage to the species as a whole. Although it is basically the females which bear the heaviest load in the pride, the responsibility of the males is equally vital. Observers have noted that without defenders the pride disintegrates, and the young are attacked by other carnivores.

The females, however, are responsible for

finding food and usually hunt during the night, though the males do occasionally help with this task despite the hindrance of their weight and flowing mane. The males may also take on the specific hunting role of frightening the prey into the ambush laid by the females. As soon as the prey has been caught the lions eat their fill on the spot, following a rigid hierarchical pattern with the adult males eating first, then the females, and lastly the young cubs. Natural selection is again in evidence, immediately eliminating the weakest animals who are unable to maintain their position in the competition for food.

The females usually become pregnant in spring or autumn, although they come into oestrus during the whole year, at intervals of about two and a half months. Following the birth, which takes place about 198 days after mating, each lioness spends her time taking care of her litter—generally three or four cubs. She normally leaves the pride either alone, or accompanied by an older female who acts as a dry nurse, sometimes staying with the mother for a few days after parturition, and helping her to hunt and take care of the cubs. The cubs begin to find their feet a few weeks after birth, stepping outside the den now and then under the watchful eye of the mother who will only leave them in order to forage for food. This is a most dangerous time for the young cubs, and they are often killed by hyaenas. 'Infant mortality' is often very high, since on average only some 50 per cent of the cubs reach maturity. A striking fact, but one of frequent occurence in the cat world, is that the mother herself eats any cubs which may have been killed and then abandoned by another predator. Only if the cub breathes or moves, or searches for the mother's nipples, is the key stimulus provided which then triggers the most attentive mother care. When the opposite occurs her predatory carnivorous nature comes to the fore.

During the early part of their life the cubs have a light, two-toned, brown coat. This pattern probably recalls an earlier period when the precursors of the present day lions possessed a variegated protective colouring, as do the majority of the present day cats.

When about ten weeks old, the young lions join the pride and the adult males sometimes take a small part in caring for them. They protect them and they may have a role in training them for the hunt. This training begins with those special 'games' of simulated attack, thus inciting the cubs predatory nature, and also teaching the various moves needed in the attack procedure. When they reach the age of 18 months the attitude

of the adult males becomes intolerable to the young lions who, being already well aware of the extent of the pride's territory and having by now learnt the required hunting techniques, are compelled to fend for themselves. Only the males, however, leave the pride.

It should be remembered that lions often hunt at night by ambushing their prey. Although able to attain a speed of almost 60 km per hour (40 mph) they cannot sustain this top speed over any great distance. They suddenly leap on their prey, and a smaller animal has little chance to escape as the lion holds it firmly down by the rump and tears at the neck. In Africa the preferred victims are, in order, gnus, zebras, gazelles, impalas, and giraffes. However, it must not be generally assumed that all of these beasts easily fall victim to the claws of the lioness. On the contrary, unless they are sick or enfeebled, their much greater speed gives them an excellent chance of escape. It follows that the lion, and, in fact, all the big cats, play an important part in the so-called selection process. The predator involuntarily helps to maintain a vigorous population of ungulates by killing unhealthy beasts.

The lions also act as scavengers on the savanna, as they are perfectly happy to eat carrion which they will even steal from hyaenas, and in fact this reversal of roles has become widespread in the Serengeti. After having eaten, the lion usually takes a long sleep. It has been calculated that during the whole day the lion spends about four hours in activity and 20 hours in sleeping, dozing, and yawning!

In spite of their notoriety in the past, lions are not normally dangerous to man, except during their stormy courtship period when the solicitous males spend all their time following and caressing the females which, conversely, respond irritably and apparently angrily, replying to the male caresses with bites and blows. A male lion scorned in love can be a decidedly intractable creature!

The Cheetah
The African savanna and the Asiatic plains are the hunting grounds of a most unusual cat, the cheetah, *Acinonyx jubatus*. Slim and elegant, it is the fastest runner of all the mammals. The lion is quite often satisfied to attack sick and weak animals, and will even eat carrion. The cheetah, on the other hand, does not always attack the weaker animals, and even the fittest gazelle may find it quite difficult to escape when the cheetah unleashes itself for the attack. It is a most powerful runner because of its exceptional anatomical adaptation. The aerodynamic silhouette

Below: A pair of cheetahs. Wild cats still play, even when fully grown

Animals Animals/T. Fuller

presented by its body, the harmonious musculature, long, sinewy legs and tough, non-retractile claws, which grip the ground firmly, facilitate the cheetah's graceful bounding action. The cheetah's body is extraordinarily flexible due to the elasticity of the vertebral joints of the lumbar region, and it is able to gather itself together and then stretch out to the fullest extent, thus increasing the length of its pace to the utmost.

It is well known that the cheetah can attain a speed of 112 km per hour (70 mph) from a standing start, but unfortunately this tremendous effort of speed demands considerable output of energy, and the animal cannot sustain it for much more than 400 m ($\frac{1}{4}$ mile). In Africa its preferred prey is either Thomson's gazelle or the impala but, if need be, it will content itself with something much more modest such as the hare.

An unusual characteristic of the cheetah as compared with other big cats is its preference for twilight or early morning hunting. This may be because its night vision is not as good as that of other members of the cat family, though this is not proven. Lying in the shade of an acacia on the savanna, its thickly spotted coat blending with the almost identically spotted shade of the tree, the cheetah carefully follows every move of the grazing gazelles. It may approach its prey immediately, without pausing, rapidly accelerating from a trot to a gallop. Alternatively, it may stalk its prey by moving forward very cautiously towards the herd, stopping suddenly and remaining completely immobile at the first sign of restlessness on the part of the gazelles. Then it continues to creep forward, still stopping occasionally, until it reaches a point within striking distance of the herd. It now selects one of the gazelles, quite often one which has become

Marka

rather isolated from the herd, and suddenly lunges forward in the direction of the chosen animal. The gazelle tries to avoid the big cat but cannot escape, and finally the cheetah bounds onto the beast, pins it to the ground and sinks its teeth into the throat. Although the cheetah normally hunts in silence, during the attack it may emit a characteristic metallic screech, which rather resembles the cry of a bird.

The distribution of the cheetah in Africa corresponds roughly to that of the lion. However, since the former can be tamed to some extent, especially when young, and also because its beautiful skin is much prized, this cat has been overhunted by man and is now extremely rare. It has been exterminated in northern and southern Africa but is still relatively common in some of the East African national parks.

The cheetah is also slowly disappearing from Asia, either because it is being overhunted or as a result of the degradation of its natural environment. India was formerly an ideal country for the cheetah, but it has not been seen there since 1948.

Apart from man, the cheetah's natural enemies are the lion, which it greatly fears (especially as it will often steal prey just as it has been struck down), the leopard, and even the hyaena and the African hunting dog which lie in wait and attack cheetah cubs. Quite often a mother's entire litter is killed by hyaenas. Fortunately for the conservation of the species, however, the nursing mother can become pregnant again, only a week or so after the cubs have been killed.

In Africa, the cheetah finds itself in constant rivalry with both the leopard and the lion for its food, to such an extent that some ecologists call this situation 'food warfare'. This is due to the

Above: A group of cheetahs. 'Infant mortality' in these animals is extremely high, as they are prone to rickets and bone decalcification

Above: A cheetah surveying his hunting territory from an excellent vantage point

fact that all three species devote their attention to a similar range of prey. In practice this rivalry is not quite so merciless as it may at first appear, especially when the supply of herbivores is plentiful. The rivalry is also less acute between the leopard and the cheetah because their chosen grounds in the savanna differ slightly. The cheetah prefers open areas where vegetation is scanty, while the leopard chooses the forest

fringes, provided that they are sufficiently wooded, and thick bush country.

The hazardous nature of existence is, of course, a fact of life for all wild animals. The main disadvantage for the cheetah is that it is a cat of daytime activity which likes to rest at night, just when the lions, hyaenas and leopards are most active. By living in the open savanna, the cheetah has partly solved its survival problem. Firstly,

Right: The large size of its captured prey is evidence of the cheetah's strength and skill in the hunt

the open spaces afford the animal the opportunity to run for long distances when hunting gazelle, and secondly, at least during daylight, the absence of large obstacles gives it the chance to spot the presence or arrival of other predators.

On the savanna the cheetah can cover long distances; it is a superb runner over short distances and is therefore not restricted to a specific territory—in fact the same area can be used by numerous individuals not normally native to it. Although cheetahs can adapt well to living in small family groups in zoos, in nature they live a solitary life and only when young do they gather together in family groups. During this time they become very much attached to a territory, and at most move from one fixed lair to another.

Delicate, subject to rickets and bone decalcification, the young cheetahs are difficult to rear and it is not unusual for the father, who is always attentive to the female, to help feed the young by chewing their food into more manageable lumps and thus make it easier for the cubs to eat.

The cheetah also urinates on vegetation, but probably not so much to define territorial limits as to signal to its partner during the mating season.

The Leopard

Among the wild cats the leopard is unusually varied both in the colour of its skin and in its size. There are a great number of subspecies of *Panthera pardus*, both in Africa and Asia. In Africa it seems that there are at least 17 different races of leopard, one of which is the Somali leopard, distinguished by its smaller size and the beauty of its gleaming, light reddish fur. It has been suggested that more than 10,000 leopard skins were exported from Somalia each year before the beginning of World War II. This was, indeed, a real butchery of a cat which, though it has the reputation of being the most fierce member of the cat family, very seldom attacks man.

To avoid confusion we must make it clear that the panther also belongs to the same species, *Panthera pardus*, the word 'panther' being commonly used to indicate the Asiatic leopard. The panther is recognized as belonging to the species because of its characteristic spotted pattern on a deep yellowish ground. On the back and flanks the markings are in groups of four or five darker, ring-like spots, in the form of a rosette.

Right: To avoid attack the leopard will climb to considerable heights, even up sheer tree trunks

Below: A leopard shows complete indifference to the proximity of the photographer

Colorific/T. Le Goubin

Bruce Coleman / N. Myers

Melanistic types are by no means rare in Asia, these animals having dark coats with barely distinguishable rosette-like markings. In other words they are the famous black panthers, which are found in some numbers on many of the islands of Indonesia.

We have included the leopard among the savanna cats, but the savanna is only one of many habitats to which this animal can adapt. It is widely distributed, and is even found in the barren African and Asiatic mountainous regions, although it is more frequent in forested areas where its innate tree-climbing ability can be used to the full.

Irrespective of its habitat, the leopard hunts by lying in ambush for its victims, both by day and night, tackling a great variety of animals. It does not scorn birds, and quite often attacks both the arboreal and terrestrial monkeys. In any

event, its speed of movement and its agility are quite exceptional.

It usually seizes the neck of its prey with its teeth, fracturing the cervical vertebrae, and then drags the carcass to a quiet spot to begin its meal. If the victim is too large to consume in one meal, the leopard pulls it up into a tree well away from hyaenas and jackals.

Little is known of the reproductive habits of this big cat, as courtship and mating both take place in the depths of the forest away from prying eyes. The actual mating is probably very stormy, with courtship consisting of scratching and spitting rather than tender caresses. When mating is completed the female leaves her partner and awaits the birth of her cubs, which she carefully rears, defending them tenaciously, and becoming more suspicious, apprehensive and irascible than ever.

Above: The clear, golden gaze of the leopard adds the final and sometimes frightening touch to the beauty of this wild cat

Smaller cats of the savanna

The necessary relationship between predator and prey is not confined merely to the big cats and the herbivores. It also occurs with the smaller cats, in this case those of the genus *Felis*, whose prey consists of still smaller animals, some of which are predators themselves.

We now propose to discuss the smaller cats of the savanna, all more or less similar apart from their variation in size. We will begin with the most common, the African wild cat, followed by the serval, the caracal and the black-footed South African cat.

The small **African wild cat** (*Felis libyca*), which some consider to be almost identical to the European wild cat (*Felis silvestris*), is common throughout the African savanna and is probably the progenitor of the domestic cat. In fact, *Felis libyca* mates relatively easily with the feral cat (a tame cat run wild). *Felis libyca* is widely distributed throughout the African continent wherever the savanna extends, irrespective of whether it is wooded or not. It presents a complex variety in one characteristic—the colour of its coat. Depending on the local population this may range through grey on a buff ground to an ochre shade. The darker, transverse stripes are rather ill-defined and merge into a lighter, spotted pattern. Even in the African wild cat it seems certain that the pelage shade is closely related to the animal's characteristic habitat, representing

Bruce Coleman / N. Myers

Right: Ever vigilant, this serval rhythmically beats the ground with the tip of its tail, signalling its excitement

a clear example of adaptation to a physical environment. As a general rule the inhabitants of the wooded savannas, although living on the forest borders in a shady and humid environment, are usually darker than those living in the grassy, arid, sunburnt savannas. *Felis libyca* is usually a nocturnal animal, and during the day hides in bushes and vegetation, sometimes in small natural holes, where it is less visible. With its colouring, it blends easily into the background.

It is a good hunter, although not specialized in its choice of prey in the sense that it has a rather wide variety of animals to choose from, including birds, snakes, lizards, rodents and even young antelopes. Occasionally this wild cat penetrates into villages at night to catch domestic creatures such as chickens, but without causing too much annoyance. When more substantial prey is harder to find it will feed on insects or even fruit.

Our second example of the small cats of the savanna is the **serval** or African leopard cat (*Felis serval*), which is much larger than the African wild cat, or the domestic cat. It is slim and elegant and it is found not only on the open savanna, but also where vegetation is denser, sometimes even living in the forest. It adapts easily to high ground and can also be found on the heaths which vaguely resemble the savanna. It is found all over Africa with the exception of the Sahara and the extreme south of the continent, and has a similar distribution to that of the African wild cat. Its food ranges from reptiles to small antelopes. There is little doubt, however, that the serval has an advantage in the vital struggle for sustenance as it is adaptable to a much wider variety of habitats. Moreover, while being essentially terrestrial, the serval climbs well and can reach the top of high bushes when hunting for fledglings. It will often eat birds and sometimes catches them in flight, lunging forward in very long bounds. It may also attack domestic fowl, indiscriminately tearing into them in a veritable butchery. Finally, although it is mainly a nocturnal animal, it can adapt to hunting during the day.

There are at least two different varieties of this species, distinguishable only by the pelage colouring. Firstly, the true serval, identifiable by a series of dark stripes on a brownish-yellow background, starting from the neck, fanning down over the shoulders and merging over the flanks and back into a series of well-marked and rather large spots. Secondly, the servalina (small serval), which is restricted to the western regions of Africa where it can co-exist with the true serval. Its typical habitat is the rather humid type of well-wooded savanna, with high, dense vegetation,

Bruce Coleman / N. Myers

and the stretches of forest on the borders of the savanna proper. It was previously considered by zoologists as a distinct species, and can in fact be found in older manuals under the name of *Felis servalina* or *F. brachyura*. The variation of colouring between the two animals is, however, minimal and insufficient to justify separate identification. The general characteristics are the same, except that the basic colour of the pelage of the servalina tends to grey with the darker spots irregularly distributed, smaller and less pronounced than in the true serval. This gives the impression that the spotting in the servalina is less distinct. Although rather rare, melanistic servals and servalinas do exist.

Servals usually mate in spring and, after carrying for about 70 days, generally produce three or four young in a den hidden among the high grasses of the savanna. If it is reared carefully, the young serval can be tamed to some extent.

Another large and robust cat which is typical of the savanna, though not only in Africa, and is never found where vegetation is dense, is the

caracal (*Felis caracal*) which is often called the caracal lynx, since it is often classed with the lynxes.

The caracal's size and principal characteristics are similar to those of the northern lynx, with fairly thick, soft fur of a uniform colour without spots or stripes. Its habitat extends from the east of the African continent through Arabia as far as India. It is a rare animal and is not often seen as it is usually nocturnal in habit. It lives in broken ground where it can hide between boulders during the day, and where the young can be carefully hidden in crevices between the rocks, or in tree cavities.

It usually hunts small mammals such as rodents and small antelopes, although it is perfectly content to eat lizards when better prey is lacking. Birds, however, are its preferred food, and when by chance it comes across a group of guinea-fowl, it bursts on them at such a speed that several of the birds are struck down even before they can take flight.

In the arid southern African regions, where no servals or caracals exist, where lions are not seen

Jacana/A. Visage

and the leopard is extremely rare, another representative of the cat family is found, in addition to the true African wild cat. This is a very small cat, known as the **black-footed cat** (*Felis nigripes*) because of the obvious black colour at the base of its paws. Although slightly smaller than *Felis libyca*, it is sometimes confused with it, at least at first sight; *Felis nigripes*, however, is easily identified by its distinctive pattern of black spots and stripes.

It is quite a rare cat, not so much due to ruthless hunting by man, but perhaps because compared to the bigger wild cat it is at some disadvantage in the struggle for survival. Due to its rarity little is known of its behaviour. It is not often seen, since it remains hidden in cavities in the earth, or in old ant-hills. It probably feeds on small rodents, especially squirrels, and birds or small reptiles.

Cats in other African regions

The typical wild cat of the humid West African equatorial forest, the only cat which can penetrate the thick, interlaced jungle undergrowth, is the big **African golden cat** (*Felis aurata*). In Asia

Above: Erroneously considered as dangerous for many decades, the European wild cats have been mercilessly hunted and, despite their cunning, few individuals have survived

Above right: The golden cat is very difficult to observe in its natural forest environment

Right: Like all small species of wild cats, the sand cat is a fierce enemy of the rodents. Its preferred prey in Africa is the jerboa

there is a very similar cat, *Felis temmincki*, or the golden cat of South-East Asia.

Felis aurata is as big as a serval but more heavily built, and is well adapted to the forest environment where it has evolved. Geographically it is confined to the humid forest areas, and is therefore limited to a narrow strip of central and western Africa. It is difficult to determine the behaviour patterns and dietary habits of the golden cat. Although it is certainly not a very rare cat, it is naturally shy and difficult even to catch a glimpse of because of its forest environment. Additionally, it usually moves at twilight and by night. It hunts rodents and, of course, birds.

On the fringes of the Sahara Desert, an entirely different environment from that described above, with little vegetation and an extremely dry climate, there is another representative of the cat family, the only one which has adapted itself to such extreme conditions. It is also found in the desert regions of Arabia and Turkestan. Its common name, significant in itself, is the **sand cat** (*Felis margarita*). It is a very small cat with rather pale colouring, obviously a protective adaptation to its desert habitat. The ear-flaps are highly developed in order to disperse the heat and the pads on the paws are almost completely covered with fur. In desert conditions it can only be active at night. During the day it generally remains hidden in sand-dune holes or under some withered bush.

Cats of the Asian forests

The tropical Indo-Malaysian forest covers a large part of southern and South-East Asia. It is one of the richest and largest forested regions in the world, extending across the Equator between the two tropical zones. Environmental conditions are typical of the tropics, being dominated by the continually high temperatures all the year round. The nearer the approach to the Equator, the more consistently these high levels are maintained. Humidity is also high but its level tends to be more variable than the temperature, especially among the forests near to the Tropics. As is well known, the rainfall in these regions is extremely heavy, but the rainy seasons come only once or twice each year, alternating with very dry seasons. The heat and humidity favour the growth of dense and luxuriant vegetation which grows again rapidly after any fires or deforestation that may occur. Such conditions provide the ideal ecological environment for the development of a varied and highly specialized fauna including, for example, the multi-coloured birds, many species of monkey and many other large and small mammals living in the trees and undergrowth. Among the animals in these areas are several species of cats, apart from the leopard already mentioned. There is the tiger (*Panthera tigris*), which is distributed over roughly the same Asiatic regions as the leopard. The clouded leopard (*Panthera nebulosa*) is also represented

Below: The colour of the Asian leopard cat's eyes varies from yellowish-green to ochre-brown

Jacana / J. X. Sundance

here, as well as a whole range of smaller cats belonging to the genus *Felis*. All these cats are good hunters, and, with the exception of the tiger, which is too heavy to climb well, they are all good climbers. They are also all solitary animals.

The jungle cat (*Felis chaus*) is also known as the marsh cat. It is a small animal (7–8 kg or 16 lb) mainly distributed in South-East Asia. It prefers the open regions of the tropical forest, but can be found in the thickets scattered among the grasslands where it hunts birds. *Felis chaus* is also found in Africa, but there it is limited to a relatively small and circumscribed area, namely the aquatic environment of the Nile delta and the lower stretch of the Nile valley itself. The fishing cat (*Felis viverrina*) has partially webbed digits and lives in marshy regions or along the water courses which run through the forest zones of India, Indo-China and the Malay Peninsula. Despite its name, evidence of its fishing habits is scanty and not generally accepted.

Felis planiceps, or the flat-headed cat, has the same habitat, diet and behaviour as the fishing cat, and is found in Java, Sumatra, Borneo and Malaya.

Above: The flat-headed cat is rarely seen, for in the forests of Malaya, Borneo and Sumatra it is active only at night

Ardea Photographics / K. W. Fink

Right: The leopard cat's kittens hide in any hole they can find, between rocks, under bushes or in small cavities

Other jungle cats include Temminck's cat or the golden cat (*Felis temmincki*), one of the few cats with a uniformly brown coat. Apart from the two black stripes on the cheeks this cat has no particular markings. It is found in South-East Asia and Sumatra. The Bengal cat or Asian leopard cat (*Felis bengalensis*) which is more widespread than the golden cat in southern and South-East Asia (throughout India, the Malay Peninsula, southern China and the Indonesian islands), preys on rodents and birds. The marbled cat (*Felis marmorata*) has a proportionally longer tail than the other small cats and a very attractive marbled coat. It is found in Nepal, Sumatra and Borneo.

Although it is rather rare, the clouded leopard (*Panthera nebulosa*) is found in tropical Asian forests, especially in South-East Asia, Sikkim, Nepal and southern China. It is midway in size between the true leopard and the smaller cats typical of the genus *Felis*.

Some authorities classify this animal as the sole member of the special genus *Neofelis*. In the play of light and shade in the jungle the colours of its fur blend easily with the shadows. It has a yellowish background with large, grey, dark-bordered spots giving a cloud-like appearance, hence its name, the 'clouded leopard'. It is a beautiful, fairly large cat and, when caught young, has been known to adapt to domestic life, hardly ever being aggressive towards man.

Living a solitary life in trees and, in spite of its size, moving from branch to branch with much agility, it generally catches birds, but by no means scorns small mammals. It can easily adapt itself to low temperatures and is found at heights of 3,000 m (9,000 feet) above sea level. Little is known of its behaviour during the reproductive period; all the observations carried out to date have been made in zoological gardens where the females normally have litters of one to four cubs.

The Tiger

The tiger is the best-known big cat of the Asiatic jungle. Until the nineteenth century it was widespread from Turkey to China, but today this species (*Panthera tigris*) is near danger of extinction, with only some few thousand specimens remaining alive in much reduced areas in India, south-western Asia, Iran, Manchuria, Malaya and Indonesia.

It would be relatively easy to repeat for the tiger much of what we have already said about the leopard, with which it shares a similar area of distribution in Asia, although the tiger extends further north. However, we must stress that the

Above: The clouded leopard is an exceptional climber. It has a long tail which is very useful as a balancing organ

Right: The strong head, lean powerful body and clawed feet of the tiger can be clearly seen in this picture

Left: Despite its huge size the tiger is a very agile animal. It can cover up to 6 m in one bound and jump effortlessly over obstacles 2 m high

Right: A Siberian tiger in its natural habitat

Right: An Indian tiger in the jungle undergrowth where its colouring provides excellent camouflage

Right: Many kinds of cats are quite fond of water, and swim with ease

Ardea Photographics / R. H. Waller

tiger is a much bigger animal. In fact, together with the lion, it shares the distinction of being the largest and most powerful of the predators. It usually fells its prey, even a large beast, before seizing it with its fangs and biting its neck or throat to kill it. Yet, like most cats, it lacks the stamina to run well over a long distance, and therefore usually hunts at twilight or at night, concealing itself carefully in the undergrowth, and getting within 10 m (30 feet) or so of its prey before making a surprise attack. Its preferred victims in India are the deer, wild boar, antelope, buffalo and sometimes domestic cattle. Occasionally some imprudent animal passes near to a tiger resting during the daytime away from the glare of the sun. One huge leap is sufficient to surprise the unwitting victim. In the same way it is by no means rare to see a tiger get a good meal from fish by catching, with incredible speed, all those that come within reach of its paws while it is refreshing itself in a stream or river. When it catches rather large beasts it rarely eats them on the spot, but prefers to drag them away—even for distances up to about 1,000 m (3,000 feet)—to where it can find a quiet spot to enjoy the meal. Having had its fill, it carefully hides all the remains of its victim by covering it with leaves and twigs, or even immersing it in still water, so

that no animal can detect the smell. Often it returns to feed again from the same carcass.

Male and female meet only long enough for courtship and mating. It is very rare for the pair to stay together, especially after the birth has taken place. If the male does stay, the mother watches the cubs very closely, in case he should try to eat them.

Usually tigers live alone and only come together in family groups during the actual mating period. Observations on the behaviour of tigers in the wild are scanty but it seems likely that the male tenaciously defends his own territory, which he defines by urinating on and within its boundaries. It may be that the territories of males and females sometimes overlap to some extent. The female urine has a special smell during the oestrus period and this acts as a signal of attraction to neighbouring males. Coupling is very quick in the tiger, lasting only some 15–20 seconds. It is, however, repeated a number of times a day during the oestrus period. Gestation lasts about 105 days and usually three or four cubs are born, but not all of them may reach maturity. When the young tiger is a year old it is already self-sufficient, although by no means fully grown.

We have already given details of this big cat's coat and the way in which it conceals itself. We

Above: Tigers appear to dislike very hot weather and during the heat of the day even those varieties inhabiting tropical regions normally like to stretch out in the shade where the vegetation is fresh and green

Right: The powerful muscles, swift reflexes and extremely acute senses make the tiger perhaps the most formidable predator among terrestrial mammals

can add that there are some individual animals which present marked variations from the typical tiger colouring. One rare colour variety has a lighter or whitish coat, instead of tawny, with brown instead of black stripes. This is a form of incomplete albinism. The inheritance of this form is relatively simple; it is due to recessive genes and may appear in the offspring of normally coloured parents as long as each is a carrier of the gene concerned.

The tiger, like all the other cats (with the exception of the domestic variety), is fast disappearing. A census was in fact completed in 1972. Although somewhat limited in its scope, the census clearly indicated that this particular species is inexorably on the decline, if not actually near to extinction.

The number of tigers in the whole of Asia has rather optimistically been estimated at 5,000. This shows a sharp decline since 1930, when there were some 40,000 in India alone. Today in this same region, considerably less than 2,000 tigers remain.

The situation is much more dramatic if the individual local varieties (or subspecies, as considered by some authorities) into which zoologists subdivide the species, are taken into account. We now propose to discuss these varieties which number eight in all.

The Bengal and Indo-Chinese Tigers

We begin with the two best known representatives, the Bengal tiger (*Panthera tigris tigris*) with perhaps no more than 2,000 surviving animals, and the Indo-Chinese tiger (*P. tigris corbetti*), of Thailand, Laos, Vietnam, Cambodia and western Malaysia.

We do not yet know to what extent this population has been reduced as a consequence of the Vietnam war. The forest areas were, of course, significantly reduced during the hostilities, when vast areas were burned by massive napalm bombing.

The Bengal tiger is the typical variety, being large and massive. Its short coat, with an almost cropped appearance, varies from orange to ochre, and is a uniform colour all over the body, with the exception of the paws, the lower legs, and the underparts, which are white, and, of course, the stripes. The whole body is covered with these prominent, transverse, dark stripes from the shoulders to the base of the tail. There are about 18 or 20 black stripes, some of which branch into two separate stripes part of the way along their length.

The Indo-Chinese tiger is smaller, and has a darker coat. The stripes are narrower and shorter, but more numerous.

The Caspian Tiger (*P. tigris virgata*)

This tiger is distinguished from the other varieties by its luxuriant and relatively long fur—especially in winter. Overall it is much darker, either because the coat is a chestnut colour or because the black stripes are very close together.

There are few Caspian tigers left and they are restricted to the northern provinces of Iran and Afghanistan.

The Siberian Tiger (*P. tigris altaica*)

The Siberian tiger is bigger than the Bengal tiger and has sufficiently long fur to withstand the bitter winter climate. Its coat is lighter in colour than in all the other varieties. This tiger was formerly distributed over a vast geographical area: it was found all along the Amur basin, the river at the extreme eastern border of Russia, in the northern regions of the Chinese Republic itself, and in North Korea.

Today there are perhaps 200 animals remaining in small, scattered, and isolated groups.

The Chinese Tiger (*P. tigris amoyensis*)

This variety is much smaller than the Siberian tiger. Its ground colour is similar to that of the Bengal tiger, but it is distinguished from the latter by its thicker and longer fur and by the less prominent black stripes. The Chinese tiger is also very rare, being practically limited to the river forests of the western areas of the Chang Chiang, the Blue River.

The Sumatran Tiger (*P. tigris sumatrae*)

This is a relatively small animal with closely striped fur, although the stripes are less defined than in other varieties. It was once very common in the island, but is now very rare.

The Javanese Tiger (*P. tigris sondaica*)

This variety is similar to the Sumatran tiger but has much darker fur. It is now found only in a nature reserve in the eastern region of the Island of Java, but even here the surviving animals total only six or seven at the most.

The Balinese Tiger (*P. tigris balica*)

This animal was very closely related to the two preceding animals, although perhaps smaller on average. It had a short and gleaming coat. However, this tiger is now almost certainly extinct.

Although the disappearance of several varieties within an animal species may seem of little importance to the man in the street, it is a matter of some concern to the scientist. As far as the biologist is concerned it has a serious significance,

since it means, in brief, that the long and extremely slow process of evolution has been in vain. In other words, many varieties of the tiger have disappeared with a consequent reduction in the animal's potential for adaptation to any new environment. Once more the intervention of man rather than natural causes has been the determining factor. Pressure has been applied in two distinct ways: directly, by man's ill-considered hunting of the big cats, and indirectly, as a result of his economic policies, by destroying the forest regions which are the natural environment of the tiger, and by acting as a rival predator.

The World Wildlife Fund has launched a campaign to protect the tiger. The following quotations from their literature indicate the extent of the problem and outline the initial impact of the measures that have so far been taken.

'Early in 1972 the World Wildlife Fund began a vigorous campaign to enlist the cooperation of all governments in countries where Tigers still survived to prevent the extinction of this species from Iran and the Soviet Union throughout south-east Asia to Sumatra and Java. Approaches were also made to the Western countries chiefly responsible for the demand for Tiger skins for the fashion trade. Results have been very encouraging and in some instances quite remarkable. Following the lead of the Soviet Union, the governments of India, Pakistan, Bangladesh, Nepal and Bhutan banned the hunting of Tigers and the export of their skins. The United States and Great Britain banned the import of the skins of Tigers and other endangered cats. Very few people have ever seen a Tiger in the wild, but perhaps because it is one of the best known and most glamorous of animals, public opinion has swung solidly behind the campaign to save it from extinction. H.R.H. Prince Bernhard of the Netherlands, President of the World Wildlife Fund, has now launched an international campaign to raise one million dollars to help the various governments concerned in their conservation plans . . .'

'Obviously, in protecting the Tiger it is essential to protect its whole ecosystem. This means not only the wide variety of animals representing its prey, but also the skilful management of their environment. The chosen reserves will therefore provide protection for a representative cross section of all Indian forest wildlife and vegetation, including many endangered species apart from the Tiger. By rigid control of poaching and the application of the latest scientific techniques in wildlife management, it is hoped gradually to build up populations of at least 100 Tigers in each reserve.'

Cats of the American tropical forests

The cat family is widely represented in the luxuriant tropical forests of the American continent, particularly those in Central and South America. These forests have very similar climates to those of the African and Asiatic forests.

The most widespread and well-known of the American forest-dwelling cats is undoubtedly the jaguar (*Panthera onca*), the only representative of the genus *Panthera* in this continent. As well as the jaguar there is a whole range of smaller cats, mainly arboreal in habit and belonging to the genus *Felis*. Because of their beautifully spotted coats, some of these cats are much prized by the fur trade and are commonly sold as ocelot. Several of these animals do in fact closely resemble the

true ocelot (*Felis pardalis*), mainly by virtue of their golden yellow pelage which is marked with closely grouped, dark spots. Examples of these cats are the tiger cat (*Felis tigrina*), present in the Amazon region, and the margay (*Felis wiedi*), which is found from the southern part of the U.S.A. to Paraguay and Argentina. They are all inhabitants of the forest environment.

The ocelot catches birds and small mammals, but will also hunt and eat amphibians and reptiles. It has not been properly studied in the wild, but is probably a territorial animal, defining its territory with faeces rather than urine. The male may share his territory, or at least part of it, with a female, but still keeps himself completely

Below: Carefully concealing itself between rocks and bushes the leopard cautiously creeps upon its prey, finally taking it by surprise with one swift leap

Jacana/P. Dupont

Jacana/A. Visage

Okapia

Above: Young red jaguarundi

Above right: Jaguar cub

independent of her. The pair only approach each other during the mating season. A modified form of monogamy may exist in this species, as it seems likely that the same two animals will mate with each other each time the oestrus period occurs. Unfortunately, this lovely cat has an attractive and much prized fur, and for this reason is in serious danger of becoming extinct. With the active protection afforded by the game reserves now being established, there is some hope that the ocelot will increase in numbers. Unfortunately its fur is still coveted and the demand from the fur trade encourages poachers to kill the animal for gain, even though they are breaking the law. Perhaps a more humane approach will eventually prevail, in which not only this cat, but all the spotted cats will come to be considered as a precious heritage of the earth's fauna, rather than as providers for the world of fashion.

The jaguarundi (*Felis yagouaroundi*) which is bigger than the small cats mentioned above, extends as far north as southern Texas. The coat is a uniform colour in each animal and may vary from dark shades of brown to black. It has a long body but relatively short legs. It is arboreal but is also a good swimmer, and finds its food from a great variety of sources—ranging over the reptiles, mammals and other vertebrates.

The Jaguar (*Panthera onca*)

Although a heavier animal, the jaguar closely resembles the leopard, and it has been claimed that it can interbreed with it. The jaguar has small, extra spots in the centre of the rosettes which make its coat distinguishable from that of the leopard. This species probably shared the same ancestors as the Asiatic panther. These ancestors moved over the Bering Isthmus into the New World, before the sea had separated the two land masses. When the two continents eventually separated, the geographical isolation of the two groups resulted in the evolution of separate species.

In the jaguar, the dark spots on the back and flanks of the animal join to form the characteristic rosette pattern. The fur is longer in the young and has a heavily blotched appearance. It lacks the characteristic ring pattern, which only appears when the cub is seven or eight months old.

Melanistic forms, similar to those of the leopard, also occur in the jaguar. The pelage in these cases is so dark that it almost completely masks the rosettes. Melanism, however, only occurs in areas where vegetation is very dense—perhaps because the protective colouring blends more easily with these surroundings. In any event, all jaguars prefer the tropical jungle environment

The margay (Felis wiedi) is arboreal, and an exceptionally skilful climber

H. Schultz

and in particular those areas close to river banks. They are predominantly nocturnal in habit, ambushing their prey and attacking a wide variety of animals: tapirs, capybaras, reptiles and riverside creatures such as otters and marsh birds. Some jaguars have developed an excellent technique for catching fish, and can lift a fish out of the water with one paw and throw it onto the bank. Jaguars are usually solitary animals and only come together in pairs during the mating season. After about 100 days gestation, two to four cubs are born, and the mother takes great care of them as they develop slowly. This slow growth, in conjunction with the lengthy reproductive cycle of this species, increases the risk to the survival of the species, all the more so as human hunters consider the skin a profitable one to get their hands on. All this leads to great anxiety for the safety of this inhabitant of the South American jungle, which has no other natural enemies apart from the largest of the constricting snakes such as the anaconda.

Above: Although much heavier and more powerful than the leopard, the jaguar is quite closely related to this inhabitant of the Old World

Cats of the northern forests

Forests of fir, larch, pine and birch extend round the Northern Hemisphere in an almost continuous belt reaching as far as the Arctic Circle, and in some parts beyond. They cover vast regions of North America and Eurasia, from Alaska to Labrador and from Scandinavia to Siberia. In these areas the climate is a rigidly limiting factor for animal life. Only highly specialized mammals can withstand the rigours of life with long winters and very low temperatures, where the ground is covered with ice or snow for the greater part of the year. Some of these animals, such as the bear and the marmot, sleep for long periods during the bitter winter months. Others, covered with thick fur, remain active and continue to fend for themselves, even when the temperature has fallen to extreme levels. The colour of the fur may change to white or at least to a lighter shade in winter, so as to afford greater protection against predators.

The northern coniferous forest harbours the elk, wolf and numerous rodents, to give just a few examples. These forests are also the home of the northern lynxes.

The lynxes can be distinguished from other members of the genus *Felis* by the long tuft of thin hair at the tips of the ears, and the short, thick-set tail. The northern lynx often possesses only two, instead of the usual three, upper premolars.

Right: The Spanish lynx is one of the few wild cats still to be found in Western Europe, although it is now very rare

There are some lynxes in Europe and Asia which, according to Grassé's nomenclature, are subspecies of *Felis lynx*. The largest of these is found in Scandinavia, Poland and Siberia. This is the common lynx (*Felis lynx lynx*), which was once widespread throughout most of Europe but now, due partly to the disappearance of the forest areas, but, more importantly to man's relentless hunting, is almost extinct. It is extinct in Italy where the last specimens were captured in the Langhe area of Cuneo province at the beginning of the present century. It also disappeared from France in 1822, from Germany in 1846 and from Switzerland in the mid-nineteenth century.

This common lynx has thick soft fur, which is especially long during the winter when it takes on a lighter shade. In summer it is reddish-grey, but lighter on the underside, under the neck and round the eyes. The back, neck and head are lightly spotted in brown. It has a very short, black-tipped tail.

It is an excellent climber and can run fast over the ground, moving almost silently. It usually hunts at night for medium-sized mammals which it springs on suddenly. It prefers hares, but will also eat wood grouse. It mates during the winter months and gestation lasts about 70 days, after which the female usually produces two or three young. During this period she lies hidden in a hole, often among the roots of a fallen tree.

The now very rare lynx previously distributed all over southern Europe, especially in the Iberian peninsula, is considered by Grassé to be a sub-species of *Felis lynx* and he gives it the name *Felis lynx pardellus*. Today it is confined to a few areas in Spain. It is smaller than the common lynx and its coat is a reddish colour with prominent spots. The white-tipped whiskers, which are particularly well developed on each side of the muzzle, are much more evident than in the common lynx.

There are at least two other subspecies in Asia: the oriental lynx (*Felis lynx orientalis*) in eastern Asia, and the Isabelline lynx (*Felis lynx isabellina*) found in Tibet and neighbouring regions.

The extensive North American forest is the habitat of the most beautiful of all the lynxes, the Canadian lynx (*Felis lynx canadensis*), with its magnificent and much prized silver-grey or pinkish-grey fur. The markings are limited to the dorsal regions, and give a definite smoky appearance to the pelage. The fur is longer than in all other lynxes, especially in winter. The tufted ears and whiskers, too, are more luxuriant than in the other races. It has been estimated that the varying hare (*Lepus americanus*) comprises 70 per cent of the prey of the Canadian lynx. The two species are therefore closely linked in the forest food chain, so much so, that when there are fewer hares, the lynxes automatically fall in numbers

Right: A European lynx in search of food

Below: A close-up of the European lynx (Felis lynx lynx)

and those that remain are forced to find other prey, such as mice, squirrels and wood grouse.

Canadian lynx furs are in such high demand that these animals are very near complete extinction. Unfortunately they learn only slowly and, being readily attracted by some tasty morsel or other, they easily fall into the traps set by hunters looking for some handsome gain.

The red lynx or bobcat (*Felis rufa*) is another American species sometimes found in the northern forests, but more frequently in the temperate broadleaved forests, from where it sometimes moves into open areas. It is a relatively small cat, at the most 90 cm (35 inches) in length, including the short tail. It has a reddish-grey fur, uniformly spotted in brown. It is a good climber and frequently hunts mice and rabbits.

All lynxes, irrespective of their species, are solitary animals, preferring to live in a rather large territory, which they do not hesitate to leave when food becomes more difficult to find. Occasionally the hunting areas of two individuals overlap or become intermixed without any precise dividing lines. However, even during the reproductive season the lynxes only remain together for the minimum length of time required to mate. They then immediately separate. Only the mother and her cubs hunt and live together for a certain period—not normally longer than a year. This is the only occasion that lynxes can be observed in groups.

The wild cat (*Felis silvestris*), which is native to the declining forests of the temperate European and Asian regions, rarely approaches the overall length of the lynx (more than a metre inclusive of the tail). It is a ruthless hunter of small mammals, mainly rodents, and birds. *Felis silvestris* is almost certainly not the progenitor of the domestic cat. The coat is characteristically marked by four black lines starting at the muzzle, going over the forehead, and merging into a single broad line which runs the whole length of the back down to the tail. The tail itself is marked by a series of dark, imperfectly defined bands. The body pattern is tawny or blackish-grey in colour. The general impression is that the wild cat is much bigger than the domestic cat, and this is particularly true of the head. Like some other species it has scent-glands, derived from modified sweat glands between the pads of the feet. Because of this, it is relatively easy to follow the track of the wild cat, especially as it scratches the trunks of trees with its claws, leaving behind a persistent smell, which warns any other cats in the vicinity that the owner of the territory is in the area.

Felis silvestris is solitary in habit. The male

lives entirely alone and only tolerates the presence of females when they are in season. Even the female cat drives her young away from her territory as soon as they are able to fend for themselves, although they are still small (usually three months old, when they may still fall prey to other predators). The wild cat is now somewhat rare in Britain. In Italy it has been reported in Maremma and in Calabria. In any event, it can often be wrongly identified since it is easily confused with the feral cat.

The domestic cat appears to be derived—at least in many, if not all, of its varieties—from the African wild cat (*Felis libyca*). It is a wild cat of the savanna, usually found in the luxuriant areas of northern and central Africa, although it is also found in Asia from Arabia to India, and in the Mediterranean islands of Sardinia and Corsica.

The Sardinian cat (*Felis libyca sarda*), now rare, is generally regarded as a subspecies of *Felis libyca* as its scientific name indicates.

Left: A bobcat sharpening its claws on the branch of a tree. This animal will often climb to perilous heights when not engaged in the search for food

Right: The European wild cat is still declining in numbers in the cool forests of Europe and Asia

Below: A young European wild cat. The four black stripes crossing the forehead and the characteristic ring pattern on the tail are clearly visible

The puma: a particular case

The puma is not restricted to any specific environment but shows great adaptability to diverse habitats, from the prairie and the forest to mountain regions. Precisely for this reason we have called it a 'particular case'. Because of its versatility, this big cat is distributed over a very wide area, and is not even confined to any single climatic zone as is the case with the majority of species of cats. It has been observed over practically all the New World, with the exception of the northernmost and eastern parts of North America. It even lives at heights of more than 5,000 m (15,000 feet) above sea level, as evidenced by puma tracks found at these heights in the Andes.

Felis concolor, the species to which the puma belongs, has many subspecies, each having a well-defined geographical distribution. In most individuals the coat is faintly blotched and there are always dark markings on the face. However, great variations in both colouring and size occur. The typical prey varies according to the area. The puma of the United States' forests and prairies are primarily terrestrial hunters of deer such as the white-tailed deer.

Although the pumas of the plains are often nocturnal in habit, perhaps because they are more often disturbed by man, the mountain pumas hunt in broad daylight. They are much bigger animals, and specimens have been found up to

Left and below: The puma is a most skilful jumper and, with one leap from a standing start, can land on a tree branch several metres from the ground

Bruce Coleman / R. Allin

Marka

2·5 m (8 feet) long including the tail, and weighing more than 100 kg (over 220 lb).

Both male and female have a short-haired coat which is usually predominantly dark but with a lighter, tawny shade on the flanks and underside. The muzzle, inner parts of the ear-flaps, and two small areas around the eyes are white. Gestation lasts about 98 days and can take place at any time of the year. The young cubs have well-spotted coats.

The puma does not usually represent a threat to man and can be kept in zoos where it usually breeds well. In its natural state the animal is nomadic and wanders over wide, sometimes vast, areas. The extent of the area covered depends on the richness of the prey to be found within it. In the Rocky Mountains each female may occupy a total area of some 14 square miles, and each male a still greater area.

The puma has the important ecological role of controlling the numerous rodents and herbivores, especially the deer, the gems of the United States' forests. In the first chapter, the ecological laws governing the reciprocal interplay of predator and prey, and regulating the respective numbers of both groups of animals, were mentioned. This law applies equally to the puma-deer relationship, and, for that matter, to the wolf-deer relationship. Both the wolf and puma safeguard the vigour of the deer population as they tend to kill primarily the weak, sick or lame animals. Unfortunately, both of these predators have been considered harmful by man, with rewards even being given to the hunters who kill them.

In Arizona where pumas and wolves have been practically exterminated, the deer population has now become almost overwhelming, having increased from a mere 4,000 to 100,000 head, and as a consequence of this great increase in numbers many die simply for want of sustenance.

Fortunately even politicians are now gradually acquiring an appreciation of ecological principles. This has led to the positive result that many states of the U.S.A. are slowly coming into line with Oregon which, in 1967, was the first state to introduce a law giving total protection to the puma.

Above: Puma cubs are weaned only a few weeks after birth, but they remain close to their mother for at least the first year of life

Cats of the mountains

We have already mentioned the puma, an animal which easily adapts itself to the severe climates of the highest mountains in the American continent. The leopard (*Panthera pardus*) also lives in some mountain habitats of the Old World. All the animals living at these heights have developed thicker and longer coats, enabling them to withstand the low temperatures prevailing in these regions more easily.

The mountain cat *par excellence* is the snow leopard, also known as the ounce (*Panthera uncia*). Confined exclusively to Asia, it is more than 2 m (over 6 feet) long, including the tail which is about the same length as that of the true leopard. It is found in the Himalayas and the Altai Mountains. The snow leopard can live at altitudes of 6,000 m (over 19,000 feet) and only descends to below 2,000 m (6,000 feet) in winter.

The general build of the snow leopard is similar to that of the true leopard, except that *Panthera*

Below: The leopard spends the greater part of the day resting on a tree branch which provides both a secure refuge and an ideal look-out

Left: The snow leopard has been greatly reduced in numbers in order to supply the fur trade with its beautiful pelt. These animals, because of their inhospitable habitat, do not present the slightest threat to man or his activities

uncia, because of its thicker fur, seems to be more thick-set. It is, however, in even greater need of protection than the true leopard, since it is not very widely distributed and it is such a rare species.

The snow leopard can withstand the very severe temperatures prevailing at 6,000 m (19,000 feet), because of the protection afforded by its long, thick coat. This blends with the surroundings and is much lighter in colour than that of the true leopard, having a pale grey-brown ground. The spotted coat is marked with a series of darker rosettes distributed over the back and down the

flanks. A black stripe runs over the back, from the head to the base of the long tail, which has incomplete, ring-like markings.

The mating period coincides with the end of winter, so that the birth of the cubs takes place in May when temperatures are less severe and food is easier to find. The litter usually consists of about four cubs who remain with the mother until the following autumn.

The snow leopard, like the mountain puma, is a diurnal animal, and usually rests in its den at night. Its preferred prey is the wild goat or any small mammal, which it attacks by stealth.

The domestic cat

The domestic cat, *Felis catus*, is in many ways a typical member of the family Felidae. With the wild members of the family it shares such features as a rounded skull with only a short muzzle, a total of 30 teeth adapted for flesh-eating, and a digitigrade walk in which the toes but not the heels touch the ground, the toes being armed with sharp retractile claws.

Within the cat family there can be no doubt that the domestic cat belongs to the genus *Felis*, which means that its closest relatives are to be found among the smaller wild cats, but from which species it came is not absolutely certain. This is not surprising. In the cases of most domesticated animals the process of selective breeding carried out by man in the short time (biologically speaking) of only a few thousand years has effected such great changes in shape, size and behaviour that the animals concerned have no very close resemblance to the wild species from which they were derived. In the absence of archaeological evidence it is only possible to guess at their affinities.

It is only necessary to compare the range of variations to be found among the varieties of domestic cats with those to be found, for example,

Beauty and intelligence are two qualities of the domestic cat that have helped to make it so popular as a household pet.
Below: Kittens of two types of cat, longhair and shorthair—a cream longhair (left) and an Abyssinian shorthair (right)

Bruce Coleman/G. Withers

S. A. Thompson

S. A. Thompson

Shorthair and longhair cats do not differ greatly in shape and size, but they do vary in coat length, in the colouring and markings of their fur and in the colour of their eyes.
Left: Shorthair cat with its short, fine and close coat.
Right: Longhair kitten with tabby markings. When fully grown its long flowing fur will be dense, silky in texture and not at all woolly.
Both types need daily grooming if they are to look their best

Bruce Coleman / G. Withers

among domestic dogs—ranging from the Chihuahua and the Pekinese to the foxhound and the St. Bernard—to see that cats are not an extreme case. They have been changed less in the course of domestication than have animals of many other kinds. Among their relatives within the order Carnivora and, indeed among the mammals as a whole, the species of the cat family are remarkably homogeneous. The genus *Felis* in particular contains quite closely related wild species in almost bewildering variety, and all bearing such a remarkable resemblance to the domestic cat that it is impossible to be certain precisely which of the wild species was the domestic cat's ancestor.

However, the most likely candidate is the African wild cat, *Felis libyca*. The mummified remains of an extinct race of this species have been found in Egypt, and these may have been the first domesticated cats. The fact that domestic cats can interbreed with European wild cats, *Felis silvestris*, does not affect the argument, for on one view the African and European wild cats are but two races of the same species. However it is possible that the African wild cat is not the ancestral species, or not the sole one. It may be the case that domestic cats contain at least an admixture of blood from other wild species. Those which have been suggested include the caracal lynx (*Felis caracal*) and for the long-haired domestic varieties, and perhaps the Siamese cat too, Pallas's cat (*Felis manul*).

The domestic cat which, like its cousins in the wild, is a solitary hunter, has one outstanding characteristic, its independent nature. Most domesticated animals—particularly the dog—tend to become so dependent on man that they suffer considerably if left to fend for themselves. Yet

105

domesticated cats that have become strays quickly find a place to live, usually in outhouses, deserted buildings or under bushes on railway embankments, and have little difficulty in keeping themselves clean, finding food, mating and bringing up their young.

The anatomy of the domestic cat contributes to its ability to live quite independently of man if the need arises. The shape of its shoulder bones enables it to climb easily and swiftly so that it can quickly escape when danger threatens. This climbing ability allows it to occupy a place of safety when resting while at the same time it can observe the approach of enemies.

Coupled with this ability are its fast reflexes; in a fraction of a second it can change from a state of relaxation to one of fight or flight. These reflexes assist the cat when it is falling so that it always falls on its feet. Its claws are retractile so that it can creep silently when in search of prey, but they can be brought out to be used as weapons of defence or attack when needed. The hunting prowess of the domestic cat is aided in poor light or darkness by the functioning of the slit-like pupil of the eye which expands greatly in diffuse light so that the cat can make the very best use of what light there is. It is this ability which, to-

P. Popper

gether with the reflecting layer behind the retina, gives the domestic cat its reputation of being able to see in the dark, a reputation that rests not only on the adaptability of the eye to varying degrees of light but also on the cat's sensitive whiskers and, in some varieties, the long hairs on the ends of the ears and in the eyebrows. These help the cat feel its way about in the dark very much like a blind man uses a stick, but in a far more sophisticated way.

The erect positioning of the ears of the domestic cat enables the animal to collect incoming sounds efficiently, and the ear-flaps can be turned towards the direction of sounds, improving still further the cat's already good hearing ability as well as helping it to locate accurately the source of the sound.

The Cat Fancy, made up of those people interested in breeding and improving the many varieties of cats, began in Britain in 1871 when a cat lover named Harrison Weir organized the first cat show. Breeders then began to keep detailed records of the cats they bred from the kittens produced. The Cat Fancy increased in numbers and was large enough in 1887 to support the foundation of the National Cat Club.

In America the first cat show was held in New York in the Old Madison Square Garden in 1895.

Above: Red variety of shorthair tabby displaying the rich red ground colour of its coat with its markings of darker red

Left: Tortoiseshell longhair kitten. This is a rare variety due to the difficulty in breeding it. As it grows, the coat markings become more distinct, displaying patches of red, cream and black

IGDA/Dani

As in Britain, this too encouraged breeders to keep records of pedigree, and a stud book was started by the Cat Fancier's Association in 1909. In Britain, the following year saw the foundation of the Governing Council of the Cat Fancy to control all matters concerning the Cat Fancy, just as the various national Kennel Clubs control the world of pedigree dogs.

Harrison Weir wrote a book in 1889 entitled *Our Cats and All About Them* in which he described the varieties of cats exhibited at cat shows. For each variety he drew up a list of what he called 'points of excellence'. From this emerged the standard of the varieties that we know today and the points system on which pedigree cats are judged.

It is impossible in the space available to describe all the varieties of domestic cat, but something can be said about those that are the most popular or exotic. The type for the British shorthair (which in America is called the domestic shorthair) is a short, sturdy body, short legs and tail, round head and eyes, powerful shoulders and short neck. The nose is short and straight; a stop or break in the nose line is a fault in the show ring. The coat is thick and short, and not too soft in texture.

Of the 12 varieties of British shorthair recognized for show purposes by the Governing Council of the Cat Fancy the tabby is the most numerous as a household pet. On the show bench the four varieties of shorthair tabbies are silver, red, brown and mackerel. The silver tabby that is to be exhibited needs to have a coat of pure silver (not white), with dense black markings and a tail that should be ringed. The neck rings must be unbroken. The red tabby has a spectacular appearance and pedigree specimens are of a rich red ground colour with markings of darker red. The eyes should be orange or hazel. To win at cat shows no white hairs in the coat are permissible.

The males of the brown tabby are massive when fully grown. The ground colour of the coat for show specimens should be of rich sable or brown with black markings, but with no white hairs anywhere. Mackerel tabbies are so-called because their marbled coat pattern resembles the fish of that name.

Undoubtedly the most popular of the foreign shorthairs is the Siamese which has no less than seven sub-varieties recognized for show purposes. The standard for the variety states that the Siamese should be medium in size, its body long and *svelte*, legs proportionately slim and with

Below: A beautiful black longhair with copper-coloured eyes. This variety is probably the most difficult to present in show condition because the fur reacts to strong sunlight and brownish streaks quickly appear

IGDA/Dani

the hind legs slightly longer than the front ones. Feet are small and oval, the tail is long and tapering and is either straight or slightly kinked at the extremity.

The head is well-proportioned and long, with width between the eyes, and narrowing in perfectly straight lines to a fine muzzle, giving the impression of a marten face. Ears are rather large and pricked and wide at the base. The eyes are clear and bright, oriental in shape and slanting towards the nose. In show specimens there should be no tendency to squint.

Very little is known about the origins of the Siamese variety which came to Europe from Siam (now Thailand). Here, for generations, members of the variety were Royal cats living at the palace of the King of Siam. They were not allowed to live anywhere else, but this stringent rule was waived in 1884 when the British Consul-General at Bangkok was permitted to bring a pair of Siamese to Britain. This was their first appearance in Europe and the beautiful creatures created quite a stir.

Among the more exotic foreign shorthairs is the rare and beautiful Russian Blue. In type

Russian Blues have long, slender bodies, long, thin tails, green eyes, slender legs and small oval feet. They have prominent whisker pads and a double coat which is very short, silky and of a medium blue shade. Unfortunately this type of coat is rare today. The colour of cats exhibited at shows is usually good, but the characteristic seal-like texture is not often seen.

The shorthair breeds of domestic cats like those described above have coats similar in length to those of the wild members of the Felidae family. This fact makes the origin of the domestic longhair breeds something of a mystery. No one is sure how and when they originated. There are records to show that they were first seen in Europe around AD 1580, having come from Angora (now Ankara) in Turkey. Later, other longhairs were brought in from Persia, and these longhairs were called respectively Angoras and Persians. These names are falling out of use, and today in the Cat Fancy of the English-speaking world they are officially called longhairs.

The typical conformation of the longhairs is that the heads should be broad and round, with good width between the small ears, the noses short

Intercamera

and broad, the cheeks well-developed, and the muzzles broad. The eyes should be full and round. The bodies should be stout and low on sturdy legs, with large, firm and round paws, and the fur long, thick and silky in texture. The short full tails should not taper.

Of the longhair varieties the whites and the blacks are the oldest, appearing at the first cat shows in Britain in their own classes. The blues, creams and reds (the reds were formerly known as oranges) were developed later as separate varieties. In spite of being one of the oldest of the five, the blacks have never appeared at cat shows in great numbers, possibly because they are one of the most difficult of all the longhair varieties to present in top show condition. The fur reacts quickly to strong sunlight and damp, and brownish streaks seem to appear almost in a day.

The original longhairs, the Angoras, were white with blue eyes and suffered frequently from deafness. There are also whites with odd eyes, one eye orange and one blue, and sometimes they can hear on the orange side but not on the blue. Others have perfect hearing. It is also possible to have whites with orange eyes.

Because of the difficulty in its breeding, the tortoiseshell longhair variety is a comparatively rare cat. The long flowing coat should have clearly defined patches of red, black and cream. These patches should be entirely free from white hairs and tabby markings, and should be evenly distributed all over the body with the legs, tail and head being patched, including the tips of the ears.

A very striking longhair variety is the Birman, often called the Sacred Cat of Burma. Although a longhair, it has the colouring characteristic of the Siamese with pale body colouring, dark points (points are mask, ears, legs and tail), and the additional attraction of four white paws. The nose of the Birman is longish rather than snub, and, in the American standard for the variety it is referred to as Roman.

The body fur is creamy-golden in colour, with the points showing a darker colouring. The points may be seal (a definite dark brown); blue (a bluegrey); chocolate (milk chocolate); and lilac (a lilac-grey). The deep blue eyes vary in intensity according to the colouring of the points.

Cat lovers insist that the many varieties of domestic cat all have different characteristics, that some make better mothers than others, that one variety shows more affection for its owner than another, that some are home-loving and others prefer to wander far afield. Each variety has its supporters, and throughout the Cat Fancy in the western world there are many societies devoted to furthering the interests of the cat of their choice.

Above: A litter of tabby shorthairs. Delicate pencil markings run down the face; there are markings like spectacles around the eyes and an 'M' on the forehead. This is the required pattern for all tabbies

110

The taming of wild cats

The domestic cat is now thoroughly adapted to the human environment. Centuries of selective breeding by man have produced a truly domesticated species. Although individuals of other species may sometimes be 'tamed', they are never as tame or as trustworthy as domestic cats, and because of their unpredictability they cannot be regarded as in any way comparable to a household pet.

There are, none the less, some cats which, in exceptional circumstances, it is possible to tame. Some species, in fact, may have acquired familiarity with man even before the common domestic cat. A case in point is the caracal lynx (*Felis caracal*), the elegant and aggressive Afro-Asian lynx used by the Ancient Egyptians in the

hunt. Evidence of this can be seen in Egyptian bas-reliefs, and in the mummified remains found in the tombs of the Pharaohs. Today, the caracal is still considered to be a good companion on the hunt, provided that it is treated with a certain degree of caution. It is still used in India to hunt deer, hares and even birds.

The serval (*Felis serval*) will accept the same food as the domestic cat. With its long, sinewy legs, it is an extremely agile animal. The natural habitat of the serval extends over all the wooded savannas, even at heights of up to 2,000 m (6,000 feet). It has to be caught young if it is to acquire confidence in domestic surroundings. In these cases it will sometimes even accept the domestic cats already there. The adult serval,

Marka

Right: If caught young and reared with care the ocelot may become very gentle and affectionate towards its owner. Its disagreeable smell, however, presents an almost insurmountable obstacle to its acceptance in the home

111

The cheetah (left) and the serval (above) have both been 'tamed', to some extent, by man

however, is a much more difficult animal to handle.

In spite of its cunning and strength the cheetah (*Acinonyx jubatus*) is undoubtedly the wild cat which has been most frequently tamed. The cheetah is a most fascinating animal and a swift hunter. It was used for hunting, along with the caracal, by the Ancient Egyptians, the Mongol princes (who used great numbers of them), and the noblemen of the European Renaissance period. In the more recent past the cheetah has been used for similar purposes in India. Most strangely, and contrary to all expectations, only adult cheetahs accept and respond well to training - never the young.

This animal has, on occasion, been kept in private houses. A very tame cheetah may accept the leash without demur when one wishes to take it for a stroll, and may even purr when stroked. It has a typically melancholy expression, which derives from the two black bands which extend from the eyes to the angles of the mouth. Only when dogs or other kinds of cats are near does it get excited.

The list of wild cats which can adapt themselves to daily life with man—although they do not by any means become truly tamed—can be extended to other species. The Asiatic clouded leopard (*Panthera nebulosa*) is one example of a cat which can be tamed to some extent if captured when very young. Considering its size, and the appearance of this beast, which hardly inspires confidence, the surprising fact is that it will sometimes behave in a relatively gentle fashion.

An Italian writer has reported a rather surprising event. It seems that in certain situations the clouded leopard will behave just like a big playful cat and will even refrain from attacking domestic animals, even though in the natural state it would certainly not treat them as friends but rather as prey.

The story goes that an animal of this species, put on board a ship about to leave Indonesia for Europe, became very friendly with the dogs on board. He hardly ever left them—playing for hours on end and always carefully retracting his claws when dealing them a playful blow. However, the moment he was given a live fowl to eat he instantly became very fierce, seizing the bird and savagely tearing it apart before finally devouring it.

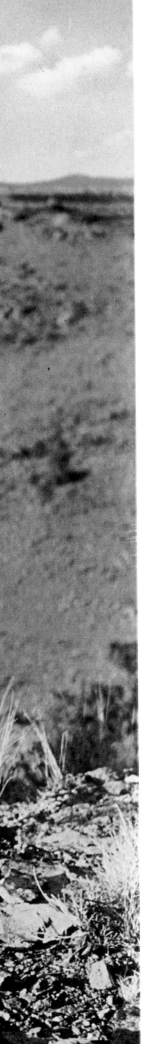

Above: A pair of cheetahs slaking their thirst

Left: Although nomadic by nature, and with a dislike of life in a restricted habitat, the puma can be tamed and rarely represents a danger to man

The puma (*Felis concolor*), which is distributed over a large part of the American continent, can also be tamed, again provided that it is captured when young. It is said that it becomes very quiet and house-trained pumas have been left to wander about in the home.

Even in the wild this cat fears man, and although in exceptional cases it will attack him, it often does not carry the attack through and the victim can drive him off.

Despite the fact that a young leopard (*Panthera pardus*) can sometimes be kept in a garden or house, it is a treacherous animal and one to be feared. As soon as it begins to get older and increase in size, it changes into a quite different animal. As with the tiger and the jaguar, once the leopard becomes adult, it is far safer to give up all ideas of pseudo-domesticity.

Several of the wild cats belonging to the genus *Felis*, apart from the serval already mentioned, can occasionally adapt themselves reasonably well, depending on the species, to a particular human environment. Unfortunately, they are very rare in nature and much more difficult to find than the serval. The following are examples of these particular cats: the jaguarundi (*Felis yagouaroundi*), said to be a quiet and docile animal which can be left free from restraint, always provided that it is kept away from domestic fowl; the South American tiger cat (*Felis tigrina*), which is much more timid than the preceding animal; and lastly the ocelot (*Felis pardalis*) which, however, is much more reluctant to make contact with man, and will only adapt itself to captivity when caught very young.

These brief remarks on the adaptability of wild cats have been added with the sole aim of providing the reader with some additional information concerning the cat family, in the hope that they will be regarded purely as such, and not as an invitation to acquire one of the more tolerant members of the cat family as an exciting companion. All wild cats are unpredictable and potentially dangerous, even when 'tamed'. It is preferable to be content with the knowledge that these animals still exist in the wild state, rather than to have them close by and irrevocably conditioned to the human way of life. We are, moreover, fortunate in having one truly domesticated species of the cat family, the domestic cat, and one need look no further for an ideal household pet, independent yet trustworthy.

The circus

The training of the big cats and their presentation as 'wild beasts' in circus shows may at first sight seem to be a matter of mere curiosity, but this practice is of interest and deserves comment.

There are some people unacquainted with the circus who think that the trainer is only dealing with overfed or even drugged animals. Nothing could be further from the truth, as the animals in the circus 'work' to the full extent of their capabilities.

Experience in the circus shows that there are some species of big cats which are more or less adaptable to training. The fierce and powerful tiger is the most difficult to handle, while the jaguar has little inclination to learn and is notoriously stubborn. The lion, despite its apparently

Marka

savage nature, adapts most easily to training. It is, after all, the most sociable of the cats, and therefore adapts itself most easily to situations involving other individuals, even those of other species, including man.

The entrance of the lions in the circus is certainly a most impressive event. This is a consequence of the tension existing between the power of the wild beast and the will of the tamer.

In all thinking people this sight must give rise to mixed feelings. Firstly, there is the initial impulse to admire the trainer's courage, as he is not only in close contact with wild beasts but must impose his will on them. But, secondly, there is a feeling of deep sadness for a beast which is so conditioned that it has been reduced to a mere shadow of the lion which literature and films have made so familiar to us.

Although the moral justification of such exhibitions is difficult to establish, the lion-tamer's tremendous self-control should not be belittled. But neither should we lose sight of the indignity of the lion, forced to leap from one stool to another, or to jump through circles of fire, actions which can hardly be considered as natural. There is more in this than man's courage, however. There is an enviable ability of the tamer to impose his will on the big cats, while knowing full well that even in captivity they have by no means lost their natural predatory instincts.

The reactions of these cats can perhaps be explained, as we have some knowledge of the laws governing their social relationships, laws which remain in force even when the circus animals find themselves in a situation far removed from that in nature. In reality it is not the animal which has to adapt itself to the new situation forced on it by man, but man himself who is constrained to predict the behaviour of the lion and become, in a way, one of them, if he wishes to impose his will. Only under these conditions will the performance unfold without difficulty. There

Left and far left: To command obedience from the group the circus trainer must first impose his will on the 'dominant' animal

Following pages: Since they are lazy by nature the big cats thrive in zoos, although it is not easy to persuade this number of tigers to share a cage

117

is no need, as many people seem to think, for the use of tranquillizers or overfeeding to render the animals docile.

As is well known, lions live in groups which are often quite large and occupy a well-defined piece of territory where they can hunt, reproduce and rear their young. The society has a precise social order, a hierarchical pattern with a 'dominant' animal—the strongest male—occupying the highest position and lording it over all the other animals. The second animal in the hierarchy gives way only to the 'despot' and is the one who lays down the law to the remainder of the animals. Then follows number three in the social hierarchy, the animal inferior only to the despot and his immediate successor, and then the remaining animals each in his place. The pride is thus precisely stratified according to the physical strength, lesser or greater, of each animal, and each individual is well aware of his position in the group.

The hierarchical order has an important regulative function and controls the total number of disputes in the pride. It has been suggested that those animals which are slow in showing respect to their 'superiors' suffer a twofold disadvantage —they come out worst in the fight, and in the competition for food within the pride, and at the same time they become more vulnerable to their natural enemies.

This social hierarchy determines not only the order of priority when the animals hurl themselves onto a captured beast to eat their fill, but also regulates the courtship preliminaries, and even the choice of a quiet spot to rest and laze during the heat of the day.

Let us now transpose this to the unfamiliar circus environment, where a group of lions are

Below: It is not unusual for two dominant lions to become bound by a quite genuine friendship, which they do not hesitate to demonstrate each time they meet, and which is not even diminished by sexual rivalry

Left: One of the most difficult periods in the life of a young lion occurs when the permanent teeth are erupting. During this time the cub loses its appetite, becomes restless and may suffer some pain

forced to live, and particularly to the cage where the lions are exhibited to the public. The cage, although a temporary home, constitutes a new territory in which the group must live. The wooden stools, used by the lion-tamer in his act, gradually take on the aspect of, and in fact represent, specific areas into which the territory is divided, each of them being reserved for one particular animal. They correspond in practice to the spot in the wild where the animal settles down to rest and, as in the wild, a rigid scale of order determined by the group is enforced.

The lions need little encouragement in settling for their own small piece of territory within the cage as this signifies a relatively peaceful zone for each animal.

In this altered situation, there is a new and most interesting element. An additional being is introduced into this small society—man, in the shape of the lion-tamer. He, from the first moment of contact, has imposed his will on all members of the group and, at this point in the performance, is just as much a lion as all the other beasts, but takes first place in the group. He is the leader to whom all owe obedience.

How does he achieve this position of power? Certainly not by mere physical strength, even though he has a whip and a stick, weapons which from experience the animals fear. His victory is almost totally psychological, and the methods by which it is achieved are security, crisp orders and intelligence. It should not be forgotten that, even between the animals, the various positions within the social scale are not usually determined by actual fighting. Often the mere assumption of attitudes of superiority and security, coupled with an exchange of symbolic gestures, is sufficient to discourage an adversary. The tamer does not

have to master and keep at bay all the lions in the group but (and here again the hierarchical scale comes into play) only the dominant animal. Once he has imposed his will on this lion, the trainer gains immediate ascendancy, and obedience from all the other animals.

Incidents may arise when the tamer ceases to maintain his position of superiority over the animals, or when he fails to notice that the relationships between the lions outside the ring have changed, and a new animal has emerged as leader.

A trainer who is unaware of such a changed situation cannot then exercise effective and direct control over the new antagonist, and may be suddenly attacked. Difficult situations can also occur when a lioness is in season, with consequent disputes between the males nearest to each other in the social scale competing for her favours. Lions in such a state of tension are very much less amenable to the tamer's attempts to assert his authority.

The oldest and youngest lions are the most dangerous beasts. Only the well-trained adults accept man as a near equal, and these will sometimes even go so far as to defend him.

The trainer communicates with the animals by movement and positioning. He will also almost certainly use his own special language with the animals, imperceptible to the spectators. This language will obviously not communicate concepts, but only his emotive state. As the biologist, Bernard Richard, has pointed out, the tamer calms and makes much of the tiger with a 'pfrr' sound, which is the same sound that these animals make when they are feeling satisfied. In the lion similar feelings are expressed by using the sound 'huaa'. Such expressions immediately convey to the animals that their master is pleased with them.

121

Cats in popular belief and legend

Ever since man's first contacts with these predators, the mystery that has always shrouded many aspects of cats' behaviour, coupled with their well-known predatory nature, has been the origin of countless myths and legends.

Among the Ancient Egyptians, the cat was so highly esteemed that it eventually became a deity —perhaps the first verifiable example in history of man's tendency to attribute to the cats, and animals in general, virtues which he himself lacked, and exceptional—even supernatural—powers. The lion was also known and respected in Ancient Egypt. It was, it seems, sometimes partly tamed. It appears on many Egyptian monuments, sculptures and bas-reliefs, and drawings of the animal have been found on the walls of tombs.

Some strange facts have been related concerning the lion in Ancient Rome. The city witnessed emperors triumphantly entering the city in chariots drawn by pairs of lions, and the slaughter of hundreds of these beasts in the Circus Maximus, merely to satisfy the sadism of the powerful, and the lusts of the people—who considered these bloody games an essential part of their way of life, as important to them as their daily bread. In fact *panem et circenses* was seen to be all that was required to keep the workless masses quiescent. The demand for lions in the circus was so great that the problem of supply from North Africa, which had experienced a consequent reduction in its lion population, compelled the government of Rome to prohibit all hunting of the animal,

Three of the biggest members of the cat family in the Old World: the lion (below), the tiger (above right) and the leopard (below right)

Left: A young lion lying comfortably in the branches of a tree

Above: A group of cheetahs lying in wait for some unsuspecting prey

S. A. Thompson

except for the requirements of the circus.

It was claimed in Rome that the lions' bones were so hard that they could be used to keep a fire burning for a long period. It was also suggested that, while the lion was a ferocious beast in the circus, it became quite calm when face to face with a woman and did not dare attack her. The Romans were also most impressed with the claws of the lion because of their obvious power to lacerate—so much so that the belief arose that during birth the cubs ripped and tore at the uterus and vagina of the lioness with their claws, to such an extent that the female could have only one litter during her life-time.

There is also a Libyan belief concerning the lion's mild behaviour when face to face with a woman, which prevailed up to the beginning of the present century. It was thought that lions were susceptible to women's pleas. One of these legends relates that women were known who had, in fact, saved themselves by imploring the lion to spare them.

According to an old Somali legend, the lion was sent to earth by God, because he wanted to punish men who had become far too curious, and made too many demands. In annoyance, God first thought to frighten them with the lion's terrible roar. But, in their initial surprise, men asked what ever could it be that made this terrible noise. 'An animal it is better not to know,' replied God. But they insisted on knowing and then God, losing his patience, sent them the lion. Henceforth they became unhappy as the beast began to kill and steal gazelles and antelopes and, more importantly, sheep and camels from their herds. Sometimes the lion even killed peasants and herdsmen.

The splendid, cunning and savage tiger has also been the source of much fantasy in the minds of simple people. Asiatic tribes have been known to refer to it as the 'human beast' or the 'superior beast'.

This relationship of tiger to man has even stronger support in the present day beliefs of the Sumatran islanders. To them the tiger is the living reincarnation of the soul of someone dead and, as such, is deeply venerated. Still stronger beliefs are held by the forest people of the Amur river region in north-eastern China, for whom the term for the tiger and for God are synonymous. Some mountain people venerate the very footprints of the tiger and, when they discover them, bring propitiatory offerings to the spot.

In India, where tigers can still be found, there

is a belief that the animals' whiskers are extremely poisonous, so when the local people find them, they are immediately burnt. In many regions, there is a strong belief in the close link between the spirit of the beast and the soul of man. Paradoxically, it is even believed that when a man-eating tiger actually eats a man the animal possesses the man's soul and is strongly protected by it. An Italian writer tells of a very strange legend.

'A tiger had killed a man and then fled. A hunter then placed the body at the foot of a tree and, armed with a rifle, waited in the tree to ambush the tiger. At night the tiger returned and the hunter got ready to fire, but the dead man raised his arm to warn the tiger of the trap. The animal fled, and the hunter came down from the tree, replaced the dead man's arm in its normal position and went back to his hiding place. The

tiger came again and once more the dead man's arm was raised to warn the animal that the hunter was hiding above. For a second time the animal's life was saved. It would have been saved a third and fourth time if the hunter had not decided to tie the arm to the dead body to stop it from warning the tiger.'

To return to more commonplace occurrences, there is also the native belief in the therapeutic powers of separate parts of the animal's body. In India for example, the fat of the tiger is considered to be a powerful remedy against joint diseases

such as rheumatism, and is also used in the treatment of animal diseases. In Siberia it is believed that eating tiger meat gives a man vigour and courage—at least enough to enable him to continue hunting tigers. The same belief is held in many parts of China where it is also thought that the animal's bones confer unique benefits, especially the knee-cap and first two ribs. The liver, too, is highly valued as a popular medicament and the teeth, worn as amulets, are thought to ward off tiger attacks or alternatively to function as charms for success in hunting the animal.

Above left: An awe-inspiring black panther

Above: The cold gaze of the Canadian lynx

Right: The cat was a sacred animal in Ancient Egypt. The bronze figure is representative of the goddess Bastet (the cat-goddess). Mummies of cats were also sacred to the goddess

Selected reading list

Boorer, Michael *Wild Cats*, Hamlyn Publishing Group Ltd., Feltham, Middlesex 1969; Bantam Books Inc., New York 1971.

Denis, Armand *Cats of the World*, Constable & Co. Ltd., London 1964.

Ewer, R. F. *Carnivores: a Full Scale Study of the Anatomy, Physiology, Ecology and Behaviour of Carnivores*, Weidenfeld & Nicolson Ltd., London 1973; Cornell University Press, Ithaca, New York 1973.

Guggisberg, C. A. W. *Simba; the life of the lion*, Howard B. Timmins Ltd., Cape Town 1960; Bailey Bros. & Swinfen Ltd., London 1961.

Harrison Matthews, Leonard *The Life of Mammals*, (2 volumes), Weidenfeld & Nicolson Ltd., London 1969 and 1971; Universe Books, New York 1971.

Morris, Desmond *Big Cats*, The Bodley Head Ltd., London 1965; McGraw-Hill Book Co., New York 1965.

Perry, Richard *The World of the Jaguar*, David & Charles Ltd., Newton Abbot, Devon 1970; Taplinger Publishing Co. Inc., New York.

Perry, Richard *The World of the Tiger*, Cassell & Co. Ltd., London 1964; Atheneum Publishers, New York 1965.

'Readers Digest' *The Living World of Animals*, London 1970.

Stracey, P. D., *Tigers*, Arthur Barker Ltd., London 1968.